"I don't know which I admire more—the down-to-earth common sense of what Tony Antin advocates or the youthful enthusiasm of his advocacy . . . His chapter on writing headlines **could change the world** if copywriters took it to heart."

> —Joel Raphaelson
> Senior Vice President
> Ogilvy & Mather Worldwide

"For years, Tony Antin has been one American we Canadians have heeded. This book provides a way to review and remember his **sound and sage guidance** which applies to local as well as to national advertising."

> —J. Douglas Utter
> Manager, National Retail Advertising
> Sears Canada

"Tony Antin's book **should be required reading** for all aspiring students. It's bound to improve their work."

> —Carla V. Lloyd
> Department Chair of Advertising
> S.I. Newhouse School of Public Communications
> Syracuse University

"The secrets of great print advertising are secrets no more! Tony Antin reveals the **fundamental principles and techniques** for the benefit of us all."

> —Peter Black
> Group Vice President, L&F Products

Great Print Advertising

Creative Approaches, Strategies, and Tactics

Tony Antin

John Wiley & Sons, Inc.
New York • Chichester • Brisbane • Toronto • Singapore

Copyright © 1993 by Tony Antin, Inc.
Published by John Wiley & Sons, Inc.

Library of Congress Cataloging-in-Publication Data:

Antin, Tony, 1923–
    Great print advertising: creative approaches, strategies, and
  tactics / by Tony Antin.
      p.   cm.
    Includes index.
    ISBN 0–471–55713–7 (alk. paper)
    1. Advertising copy.   2. Advertising layout and typography.
  3. Advertising, Magazine.   I. Title.
  HF5825.A58 1993
  659.13'2—dc20   92-27820

Printed in the United States of America

10 9 8 7 6 5 4 3 2 1

Preface

After more than a year of special "consideration" around the house, of being given undisturbed and unburdened status while all the chores of daily living got done, of having cranky expressions of author's anxieties overlooked, I now totally understand why so many prefaces start with heartfelt (or is it guilty?) thanks to one's spouse. So first and most deeply felt, I thank a woman I have called "Dear" (both proper noun and adjective) for 45 years.

Then, for the "unique opportunity to learn" that I describe in this book, I owe and write thanks to *Reader's Digest*. To Wally and his editors, whose principles, techniques, skills, and talents I was privileged to study, define, learn, and teach. (And I was *paid* to do it!) Patently, without that unique educational experience, I would have had no book to write. I thank the *Digest* also for its unlimited permission to reproduce on the following pages any and all of its copyrighted editorial material. And *Digest* advertising librarian Helen Fledderus for always finding and supplying facts and material, even when I could give only the vaguest clues.

After I did an outline of what I might write for this book, I was complimented that the publisher wanted everything I had. But when that proved to be far too much for *these* pages, my editor, Karl Weber, did a first cut worthy of the best *Digest* editor (and left me with enough to wonder if "Dear" will permit another book). That impressed me. But he *amazed* me by knowing the total manuscript so well he could, for example, suggest that we might delete something from MS page 23 because I said essentially the same thing on MS page 311; or that three lines on MS page 134 worked beautifully as the ending of a paragraph on MS page 56. And throughout our work together, because I have edited as much as I have written, I felt again—and am thankful for—the bonding that must happen before writer and editor can do something far better than either could do alone.

For any wisdom that shows in this book, I thank so many professional and personal friends who, though unknowingly, helped me to it through many hours of conversation, of bouncing ideas, of responding with perspectives that enriched my own. Stan Plog, the only Ph.D. researcher I know who understands (and retains his own) humanity; and who, through my use of his work during a major and multiyear project, convinced this skeptic that research *could* be done in such a way as to help a writer know how to "start where the reader is." Professor Dennis Martin, who, with his Beta testing mindset, prompted me to fill holes in what I had thought was already valid; and who gave me the opportunity to work with and perhaps influence college students of advertising. The late Dr. Robert E. Doherty, who taught me how to go on learning throughout life. Colin Wheildon, who has been my contributing ally in our fight against bad typography. George Grune, who, with our shared successes, taught me never to quit on a sale—to take what did not sell in one form, reshape it and try again...or somewhere else.

And for the trench work on this book, thank you, Linda Indig, for your patience and devotion; thank you, Lori Martinsek, for grasping so quickly what I preach; and you, Claire Huismann, for all your work from one FedEx package to the next.

Tony Antin
Darien, Connecticut
December 1992

Contents

Introduction

What's in This Book for You?

I base the *promises* of this book on three *premises*. You can read the premises in either of two ways: (1) In relation to yourself, with the promise that this book can help you professionally or (2) in relation to people who work for you—or whom you must teach—with the promise that this book can help you help *them*.

The Underlying Premise Too many people in advertising have forgotten (if they ever knew) the only legitimate objective of an advertisement: *To make the proposition of the advertisement quickly, easily, fully, and memorably clear.* I don't like or mean to start by offending, but possibly, without realizing it, you are among those who have "lost their way" (or never *knew* the way). If so, and if you read and think objectively and open-mindedly about what's in this book, you will come away with a new perspective. Actually, if you have forgotten it, you will recapture the original perspective on what it is all about—what we must always concentrate on doing when we advertise. Finding (or rediscovering) that new (or old) objective will help you do your job better. For the good of your company and your own career, no matter what part of the field you now work in or for which you now study. (Or, I'll say this once more, then please assume the same for the rest of this book: It will help you help *"them"*—those people who work for you or your students.)

The Second Premise Too few people in advertising know the basics of print advertising—the "mechanics" necessary to create, critique, and/or approve advertising free of needless flaws. Free of mistakes that should never occur at that fundamental level, but often do. They smack of mistakes in spelling or simple arithmetic by supposedly educated adults. Mistakes embarrassing to make and to see made . . . and so easily avoidable or correctable.

The Final Premise Too many people in advertising want to run before they truly know how to walk. Want to "paint abstract" without the ability to paint realism. Think they can produce great print advertising when they don't know (or even know the existence of) the fundamental qualities common to all great print advertising. When they don't know the tried and proved routes which advertising has taken for many, many years to reach greatness: the Creative Approaches, Strategies, and Tactics that have been repeatedly used in the past and are still used today.

To all who read and study this book, I promise:

- A pragmatic, step-by-step workbook to help assure that you never again make or leave uncorrected any of those totally unnecessary mistakes in the basics.
- An understanding of the qualities common to all great print advertising. Possibly a first-time realization that what Harry Truman said about life holds equally true in advertising: "If you think there is anything new, you don't know history." That every great print advertisement you see today uses creative approaches, strategies, and tactics that have been used before.

If you learn, as you can with this book, the approaches and strategies and at least some of the tactics, when you sit at a word processor or drawing board, reaching for greatness, you won't have to sit for hours trying to re-invent the wheel. You can "start your mental engine" by experimenting with these tried-and-proved routes to great advertising to see if one lights a bulb for the job on which you are working.

That's what I promise to *all*.

To Client-Side People

Marketing and advertising directors and managers; "groupers," product managers, and assistants; directors of advertising services—all those who work with agencies to formulate advertising directions and approve (or disapprove) print advertising in copy/layout and then in final stages, I promise you:

- A professional method for critiquing copy and layouts and for articulating your thoughts so that (1) you will never again send your agency people away knowing they must change something but not knowing what and/or (2) you will never again be sweet-talked (or out-argued) into approving something that your marketing knowledge (or maybe your human instinct) tells you is wrong.

- I promise you also a spirit-rejuvenating debunking of the complaint that "you just can't get good print anymore." This book can give you a proved-by-many-examples conviction that not only is good print done today but also, with the same frequency with which you see truly great advertising in *any* medium, you see *great* advertising in print. And *you* can learn enough about how good and even great print advertising is done (it's no mystery) to (1) stimulate and/or prod your agency people to create always good and sometimes great advertising for you and (2) possibly even help them do it.

To Agency Creative People

I have done perhaps a hundred or so seminars for agency creative staffs in the United States, Europe, Africa, and the Pacific area. I always start by saying, "If you have been creating print advertising as long as I have, you will not learn anything new from me today." And, almost always, after the session, a senior person or two will smile (often ruefully), "You were right. I didn't learn anything I have never known. But, *oh*, did you remind me of so much I forget too often!" So, to such senior people, I promise as reminders and reinforcers (and to others, I promise as career-advancers):

- To explain and illustrate the *fundamentals* of good and great print advertising in ways that (1) can make them more clear than you have ever seen them before and (2) will convince you to heed and always correctly apply these fundamentals.
- To show that, in creating great print advertising, there is more *method* than mystery. That you can learn—yes, consciously learn—how to achieve greatness more often. Or at least come closer to it.

To Agency Account Service People

I know many of you have suffered the disdain of some in the creative department who call you a "suit." But I also know well the value of marketing-minded (and client-sensitive) input during creative discussions. And, having often been the creative director worried about approvals and "trying to get the damned thing out," I value those who keep the "approvers" off my back, who take care of all those meetings, who set the right stage for presentation, and who know how to represent our work. As a creative-side person, I value *creative-educated account people*. So, to you, I promise:

- To help make you solidly knowledgeable about the basics of good and great print advertising. This for the purpose of making you more constructive, thus more welcome and *productive* in working with your creative team.
- To help make you more effective in representing your agency's creative work with clients—which should not mean simply fighting for it, but sometimes recognizing that you must go back to the "creatives" and, most important, knowing how to articulate the problem.

To Students

[Faculty: Read this "over their shoulders" to see how I hope it will help you teach them.] I hope to do *many* things for you. But I'll feel that I have given you the most fundamentally helpful service if I can shake you out of the idea that the name of the game of advertising is "cleverness." I should not even have used the word *game* there because it feeds another wrong impression: that advertising is exciting. *Maybe* you will have some fun. *Maybe*, now and then, it will be exciting. But advertising is hard—repeat, hard—and sometimes tedious (and even at times dispiriting) work. Double-u. Oh. Are. Kay.

The name of the *business* of advertising is "communications." (Yes, the objective is to sell something, but you sell nothing until you communicate. Whether it's fact or fragrance—even ambience—if it's why they will buy, it must be *communicated*.)

Perhaps the most humbling lesson we eventually learn is how little attention "those people out there" pay to our work. They would just as soon *not* see our advertisements. We have only an instant to signal something of interest to them, and then only seconds—at most only a few minutes—to communicate it all. That makes it difficult, difficult, difficult to communicate through advertising. You will have a hard enough time learning how to and then doing *that* well. Sometimes, while you work to communicate, something clever will come to you. If it helps communicate and does not detract from clarity, fine. But I want to help you where it will count most. Hence, to you students, I promise:

- A textbook on how always to communicate effectively — and sometimes with fame-earning success — through print advertising. I promise you a book filled with principles that you can understand, principles that, if you work by and never forget them, will keep you on the right track. And I promise you techniques with which to apply those principles correctly and skillfully.
- If you keep this book handy, a reference that can guide and serve you for years.

These are big promises, I know. In fact, with all the writing still ahead of me to fulfill them, I feel heavily the burden of working to do so. But I feel no uncertainty. I write this not immodestly, but with the experience of many years of face-to-face teaching and the repeated pleasure of seeing the value to others of what I have had the unique opportunity and good fortune to learn — and want, on the remaining pages, to pass on before I do.

The Unique Opportunity to Learn

1

From 1922 to 1955—for a third of a century—the *Reader's Digest* flourished without advertising in its U.S. edition. Oh, how it flourished! Making its owners, DeWitt and Lila Wallace, General Manager Al Cole, and a number of its editors very, very wealthy. All from only the 25-cent cover price of those years. (In 1950, the *Digest* started its Condensed Books, and then its record albums nine years later—both instantly popular and wondrously profitable. But, from 1922 to 1950, the "little magazine" alone, *sans* advertising, had been the prolific golden goose.)

An inside joke about advertising said that, like many Americans, the *Digest* was not above a little sinning when abroad. So it had carried advertising in its international editions since 1940, when it started *Selecciones del Reader's Digest*, in Spanish, for Central and South American readers. Of course, the real and practical purpose of the advertising was to keep the cover price affordable in those other countries. (Al Cole once told me that, with the strong Nazi presence in Argentina at the time, the U.S. State Department urged the Wallaces to publish the *Digest* there as an unparalleled interpreter of America. When announcing the magazine's international expansion in the August 1940 U.S. edition, DeWitt Wallace wrote of circulating "throughout those countries where a clear conception of the United States of today will promote an alliance of interests for the cause of peace tomorrow.")

In 1955 in the United States, the uncontrollable and continually rising costs of printing, postage, and paper began to make it less and less profitable to keep the domestic cover price at 25 cents, where it had started and stayed for 33 years. That's when Wally and Lila (as everyone called them) and some of their senior people began to talk seriously about the possibility of accepting advertising in the U.S. edition. The *Digest* had surveyed its American and Canadian readers, asking, "Would you rather have advertising in the magazine or a higher price?" The readers voted overwhelmingly for advertising. But there was never a "show-time" meeting, with all sorts of charts and data studied and a momentous decision made. Rather, one day Wally stopped Al Cole in the hallway and almost offhandedly told him that he and Lila had decided the *Digest* should start to carry advertising in the United States. As Cole and Fred Thompson, who became the *Digest*'s first Advertising Director, told me over the years we worked together, the subsequent scenario went about like this:

Thompson and a copywriter from the *Digest*'s agency, BBDO, drove to a motel in Bridgeport, Connecticut, planning to write and set, in secret, an advertisement announcing the opening of *Digest* pages to advertising. But the advertisement, pre-empted by a news leak, never ran. Within days, *Digest* telephones rang and rang with land-rush "buy" calls. Including, of course, many from BBDO, which finally got through to Al Cole with the plea, "If you won't come to us, we'll come to you. Just say when and where!"

"No," Cole said, "we'll come there. How about tomorrow about five?"

The next afternoon, when Cole and Thompson walked into a crowded conference room on Madison Avenue, a man holding a thick sheaf of orders for advertising pages interrupted their entrance. "Before you say anything," he said, "these are for you . . . for your ad director." Turning toward Thompson and pushing the orders at him, the man asked, "Is *he* your ad director?"

With a half-smile and raised eyebrows, Thompson glanced questioningly at Cole, who laughed, "Yes, he's the advertising director." The appointment and announcement made simultaneously on the spot.

The *Digest* had decided that, to keep what it considered the proper editorial/advertising balance, it would carry no more than 32 pages of advertising in each issue. By that quota, what the BBDO man handed Thompson amounted to *two years' worth of advertising!* From one agency! Foretelling that within months the quota system would be recognized as impractical. Instead, to keep its promise to paginate every national advertiser adjacent to editorial material, the *Digest* adopted a policy of adding editorial pages to assure it. (Ten years later, *Digest* readers were enjoying an average of 100 more pages per issue than they had in the *Digest* without advertising.)

Yes, one cause of the stampede for space was the allure of virgin territory. But there was much, much more to it than that. And this "much, much more" led to my getting a unique job assignment that gave me the unique years of learning experience; and which now has led me to write what I hope you will find to be a unique and uniquely illuminating book.

The New, Truly Mass Medium

In early 1955, the biggest medium in which you could advertise for a guaranteed household reach was the old *LIFE* magazine (the weekly before its present reincarnation) guaranteeing just over 5.6 million households. (Television claimed but could not guarantee more.) When the *Digest* entered the arena that year, it guaranteed over 10.2 million households in the United States (and another eight million abroad if you wanted them). Agencies and advertisers were justifiably awed by these numbers, but they were equally, if not more so, impressed with other factors:

- *Digest* editors clearly knew how to make more subjects more understandable, thus more interesting, to more millions of readers than could any other group of editors in publishing.
- Over the years, the *Digest* had earned an unmatched faith in the magazine and rapport with readers. Time and again, advertisers and agencies had seen one *Digest* article "make" a product "overnight." (A one-page article titled "It Makes Tough Meat Tender" rocketed Adolph's Meat Tenderizer to national and international sales. The first *Digest* article charting the tar and nicotine in different cigarette brands immediately made Kent the best-selling filter. Until subsequent *Digest* reports showed less tar/nicotine in other brands—and then *they* took the lead.)
- Copywriters who wanted to write better headlines had been urged to study the article titles in the *Digest*.
- The clarity and blessed brevity of *Digest* articles ranked as one of the wonders of the writing/editing world.

In short, advertisers and agencies credited the *Digest* with having a phenomenal record of mass communications and mass persuasion in print. And that led to something ordinarily inconceivable: Advertisers and agencies began to ask the *Digest*'s advice about the creative side of their advertisements. I never heard of them asking *LIFE* or *Saturday Evening Post* or any other magazine. Nor, I feel certain, had they ever asked broadcast networks or stations. But very early on, they started to ask *Reader's Digest*. Of course not asking the *Digest* to answer as an advertising expert, but rather as the proven *print communications* expert it was (and is):

> "Reader's Digest, *how do you manage always to approach a subject in precisely the way most people are most interested in it at that time?*"
>
> "*Your headlines read so quickly and easily and are so immediately and totally clear. What's the secret of that?*"
>
> "*How do you make the copy so short without losing anything?*"

At first, we, the *Digest*, didn't know how to answer. Our editors just *did* what they did; they had never *analyzed* what they did.

Unique Job Assignment

That analysis became my job, over 30 years ago: to study what *Digest* editors do to produce a magazine that attracts a Super-Bowl-size audience—100 million readers now—and not just once a year, but every month.

To study to see if any of what *Digest* editors do could be defined. Brought out as identifiable and describable, thus teachable, principles and techniques. And, if so, then to answer the critical question: "Can any of this be applied to print advertising?"

I found that all of it not only *can* but *should* be applied to print advertising. I found that the three fundamental qualities that make a great *Digest* article also make a great advertisement:

1. The article offers something (e.g., information, laughter, vicarious thrill, inspiring story) that a great many people want very much (a benefit).
2. Figuratively speaking, the instant the article "opens its mouth" with its general "look," headline, and/or

illustration, it makes that promised benefit easily, and thus instantly, seen and recognized.

3. After the initial offering, the article makes the benefit easy to get in full.

In short, short summary, a great *Digest* article offers a much desired benefit, makes it instantly recognizable, and makes it easy to get quickly.

A great advertisement has exactly the same three fundamental qualities. And I found that, right down the line, the *same* principles and techniques apply for great communicating on *both* editorial and advertising pages. It was my learning, articulation, and demonstration of these truths (over a span of many years and by no means easily) that led Hobart Lewis, then Editor-in-Chief and President of *Reader's Digest*, to say, "Tony, we just do what we do; you're the only one who can explain it."

I answered, "Well, isn't that always the case? Those who can do, *do*, and those who can't, *teach*."

"No," he graciously replied, "you can do it, too... and consciously." Immodest as it seems for me to say so, he was apparently right. Because during my years with the *Digest*, working side-by-side with agencies and companies to help produce, both for them and for our pages, the best possible print advertising, I have applied to their advertising the principles and techniques I learned (and have never stopped learning) by studying the *Digest*.

At first, I was surprised and later, for years, delighted and complimented to discover that advertisers and agencies found what I had to say and show as examples to be a unique, enjoyable, and exceptionally effective way to learn more about how to make better print advertising. It has been both very satisfying and a great pleasure to do seminars on that subject for the stimulating people in:

- Such varied companies as Kraft General Foods, IBM, and Pepsi-Cola
- Such venerable agencies as Ogilvy & Mather, J. Walter Thompson, and Foote Cone & Belding
- Countries from Scandinavia to South Africa, from Australia/New Zealand to Japan
- I've forgotten how many Advertising Age Creative Workshops
- Advertising clubs from coast to coast
- Universities such as Brigham Young, New Hampshire, and Michigan State

A New Kind of Advertising

With these principles and techniques, we also broke new ground in advertising. We, in the *Digest*'s Advertising Division, looked for companies, groups of companies, or entire industries with major problems or opportunities that might be solved or seized by a type of advertising that provided information or corrected misinformation—educational advertising with a 100% commercial purpose. The Advertising Division's Creative Department (which I started and headed) would do this advertising job "the *Digest* way." The client/agency provided *what* to say; we provided *how* to say and show it. Acting, in essence, as subcontractors for the agencies, we sold and produced, during my fully active years, approximately $80 million worth of that special advertising, often for clients and from budgets that did not exist before. For example, when the wide-bodied airplanes brought with them millions more airline seats to sell, current *Digest* Chairman/CEO George Grune (then Marketing Director) and I sold, to an ad-hoc consortium of six airlines

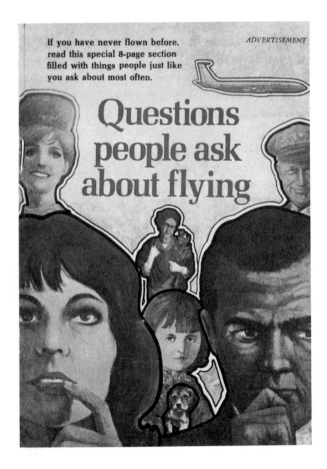

and Boeing, a three-year informative advertising program to stimulate more people to fly. The campaign used multipage booklet advertisements, such as the one you just saw, to make more people familiar with flying. Research had shown that non-flyers were unfamiliar with flying, and that people avoid the unfamiliar.

Reading what I have just written, it seems to boast and drop names, but that was not at all my intent. I wrote it simply to document for you that the principles and techniques defined, explained, and illustrated in this book are, above all, pragmatic; moreover, they have been tested and proved valid in the advertising arena. I consider it the finest compliment when people kindly say, as I'm so grateful that they do, "I can put this stuff to work tomorrow... THIS AFTERNOON! You have helped me do my job better." In writing this book, that's what I want to do for you. Let's get into it.

PART ONE

The A, B & C
of Effective
Print Advertising

How Great Print Advertisements Get That Way

2

I diagram the levels of advertising and how advertisements reach each level, as shown here. Simplified, certainly, because of course there are gradations between INEFFECTIVE, EFFECTIVE, and GREAT. Take a moment to study this diagram because it provides the "road map" for this chapter.

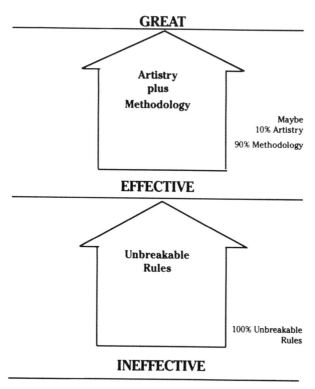

GREAT

Artistry
plus
Methodology

Maybe
10% Artistry
90% Methodology

EFFECTIVE

Unbreakable
Rules

100% Unbreakable
Rules

INEFFECTIVE

For two reasons, I don't need to define INEFFECTIVE. First, of course, you know what ineffective means. Second (and I regret having to say it), all you need do is look about and you will see examples galore.

EFFECTIVE advertising is good, is workable, does the job, and represents a significant achievement if it can be produced 100% of the time. I see no reason why normally intelligent people cannot produce EFFECTIVE advertising *every time*. But we don't, and I am not alone in knowing why.

When advertising was an infant industry, a typical scenario might have had a merchant who had just received a shipment of calico hurrying to the local newspaper to place an advertisement announcing he would have it on sale for 10 cents a yard. In those days, no one thought of advertising as having any other purpose, any other objective, than to *communicate*.

"Today," David Ogilvy has said, "the people who are paid to write advertising...consider advertising an art form. And they talk about creativity all the time." These people have in their minds what I call "cliché notions" of how a "big-league" print advertisement should "look" and be written. And when they prepare to write an advertisement they start with the wrong objective. Instead of setting out to *communicate,* they set out to *create an advertisement*—and to do it according to all their cliché notions, the primary (and most harmful) being that you must always try to be clever. In that pursuit, communicating disappears as the central objective. And *Forbes* magazine accurately reflects public reaction to so many of the resulting advertisements with an article titled, "What the hell was *that* all about?"

I can't (and don't) blame the copywriters, art directors, creative directors, account-side and client-side people who make these advertisements. They are the products of an industry with false standards, an industry in which they must swim or sink with no help. To survive, they look around to see what is passing as advertising and, especially, what wins awards. Now and then, at a conference, they may hear someone call for clarity over cleverness. But instead of following such advice, they teach themselves to imitate what they see. Some of them get awfully good at it. And, since what they imitate represents what the *industry* considers good and great advertising, they earn rich rewards (both in money and statuettes). So where is the incentive—or even a reason—to change?

What Can We—*Must* We—Do about It?

First, we must return to the conviction that the objective of advertising is to *communicate.* (I noted in the Introduction and say again: Yes, the objective is to *sell* something; but you sell nothing until you *communicate.* And "communicate" *includes* transmitting a modish message through the chic execution of an advertisement.) In addition, we must learn or relearn that people will not work to understand advertisements. Thus the burden of communicating lies totally with us, the advertising makers.

To reach the objective of communicating effectively every time we create a print advertisement *demands:*

1. Knowing, thoroughly knowing, the fundamentals of effective print.
2. Applying them in every single advertisement we create, critique, or approve—no exceptions, not in the basics.

Which means always applying those "Unbreakable Rules" noted in the diagram. I know that those words—"Unbreakable Rules"—raise hackles among quite a few people in advertising. Some simply because they cannot stand the discipline of working within rules. Them, I ignore. I don't have time for foot-stamping emotional children. But if those words raised your hackles because they honestly puzzle you, bear with me while I try to provide an explanation you might accept.

The Difference between "Rules" and "Trite Executions"

The people who urge you to "break the rules" fail to differentiate between a *"rule"* and what becomes the *"trite execution"* of it. You must not break a rule. But, if a trite execution of it has taken over, you should *always* try to break that . . . the trite execution. For example, a rule says you should picture your product attractively. In cigarette advertising, for a long time, the trite execution of that rule had three parts:

1. The package was shown as though part of the top (from end to tax stamp) had been surgically sliced open with a scalpel, not torn open by fumbling human hands.

2. Three cigarettes—never two, never four—protruded from that neat opening.

3. Each cigarette was pulled out of the package a different amount to make a nicely staggered pattern.

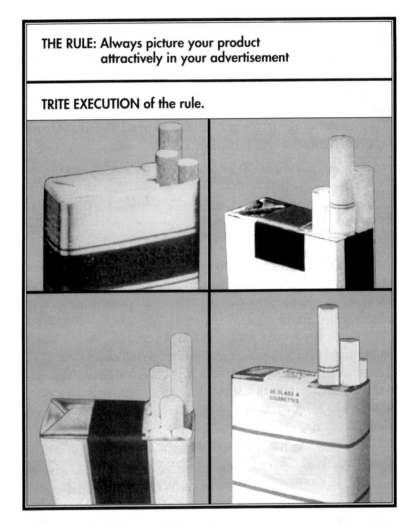

THE RULE: Always picture your product attractively in your advertisement

TRITE EXECUTION of the rule.

During an Advertising Age Creative Workshop presentation called "My Lover's Quarrel with Advertising," I showed advertisements for 12 different brands, all with that trite execution. As I punched each new slide to the screen I repeated, "Three up . . . three up . . . three up." By the fourth slide, the audience started to laugh; by the tenth, they were howling with derision. With the twelfth and last, they stood up and roared!

If your hackles were up, did that explanation lower them? Are you now amenable to reading and seeing—and considering—the Unbreakable Rules which, when followed correctly, create EFFECTIVE print advertising? Good.

The Two Parts
of Great Advertising
Performance

In figure skating, to win the gold medal, a skater must score extremely high in both the compulsory and free-skating parts of his or her program. Think of great advertising as having its "compulsory" and "free-skating" parts, too.

Compulsories The advertising compulsories are the basics, the area of the Unbreakable Rules. Great advertising demands not just high marks (9.5, 9.7); it demands *perfect* marks, straight 10s. We can acknowledge the physical impossibility of a human body, even that of a gold-medal skater, making every move perfectly every time. But, to cite one of advertising's rules (i.e., compulsories), surely it is not impossible for a human mind always to write and set an advertising headline to make it so easy to read that people read it before they actually decide to, with but an idle glance.

Free Skating It surprised me when I eventually understood that this part includes *methodology* as well as artistry. In fact, although the artistry is, of course, imperative, "free skating" requires much more methodology than artistry. I believe the proper ratio is about 90% methodology and 10% artistry. Let's use our skating analogy to illustrate: When a gold-medal skater does, say, a triple axel and lands with hands and head in positions that are breathtakingly beautiful but also breathstoppingly dangerous to balance, that's the critical 10% of artistry that makes the audience and the judges gasp and brings the 9.8 or even 10. But probably 90% of that classic leap, tri-spin, and landing is strictly delineated method. The skater must take off on a particular edge of a particular skate, must make a specified number of revolutions with body in certain positions and attitudes at each point of the spins, and so on through the specified form of landing.

We'll come back to all this in Part II, when we concentrate on the second part of how great print gets that way. But in order to get the most out of that part, we must work first on what I call "The A, B & C of Effective Print Advertising." Note the "&." Don't misread it as "The ABCs" and think we will deal with kindergarten stuff. I will work as hard as I can to make these basics clear and convincing to you, but they are no more simple than are the basics of human behavior—to which all of them can be traced.

The A, B & C	Proposition or Advertisement	EXPLANATIONS
"A"	**Proposition and Advertisement** For "this product at this time," does the Proposition start from where people are to make *The Right Offer?* Is the *first* element seen compatible with and helpful to *that* offer?	*"Right Offer"* = Strongest possible product benefit (real or perceived) to largest possible number of people. The Propositional Benefit. *"first element "*= Could be overall "look," a major illustration, a bold headline instantly read-- whatever is visually strongest... most likely to be seen/read first with just idle glance.
"B"	**Advertisement** Does it make *some* benefit instantly apparent; and The Right Offer--the Propositional Benefit--then *immediately* and *easily understood?*	*"Some* benefit"= Could be The Propositional Benefit (real or perceived) OR a Laid-on Benefit which might or might not relate to it. *"Right Offer immediately, easily understood"* = If Laid-on Benefit does not relate to Propositional Benefit (real or perceived), advertisement moves immediately into it.
"C"	**Advertisement** Does it make *everything* about The Right Offer--Propositional Benefit--*quickly, easily and fully clear?*	*"quickly, easily, fully clear"* = people able to read and understand *every*thing about Right Offer (Propositional Benefit) with no effort at all.

OFFER

The A: An Appealing Propositional Benefit

3

Every advertisement makes a *proposition*, an offer. The proposition must always urge a quid pro quo that enough of the right people will see as beneficial to themselves. Why else would they—or *should* they—accept the proposition? Or even bother to read it?

Advertisements for products or services propose that you "buy this product or service to enjoy this benefit." The benefit can be a *tangible* benefit, such as a low price, or a *perceived* benefit, such as feeling seductive because you wear a certain fragrance. Corporate advertisements should propose that you "view us this way (1) so you will know from whom you can get better products or service or (2) so you will know from which stock you might benefit, or (3) for some other reason beneficial to you. Advocacy advertisements state, "We propose that you believe these facts for the benefit of knowing the truth," or, "We propose that you take this action to do the right thing for yourself and/or for society."

Form the Proposition First You develop the proposition long before you start to create an advertisement. You must know *what* you will propose before you can start work on *how* to propose it.

- Marketing management people—or advertising people exercising a marketing function—form the proposition when they decide how to *position* a product or service. "For this product or service at this time," what position will make enough of the right people view using it as beneficial to themselves?

- Those responsible for corporate advertising form a proposition when they conclude what image of "this company at this time" will make enough of the right people view doing business with or somehow supporting the company as beneficial to themselves?
- An advocacy proposition is formed when someone decides how, for "this cause at this time," to advocate a belief or course of action so that people will see self-interest in accepting the belief or taking the action.

To save space, because we all know that it may be a (1) product, (2) service, (3) company, or (4) cause being advertised and because the principles and techniques for effectiveness are the same for all, I will simply use the word *product* from here on, meaning all or any of the four.

Most often, an advertisement spells out its proposition literally. Sometimes, however, the *creative execution* of the advertisement makes the proposition. This can happen either when a product has tangible benefits but the marketers choose to base its appeal upon intangible (perceived) benefits, or when the product has no tangible benefits. In both cases, just as people can make statements about themselves by the way they dress and act, the creative execution of the advertising makes the proposition by its appearance and attitude.

The Propositional Benefit

I call the tangible or perceived benefit derived directly from accepting an advertisement's proposition the *Propositional Benefit*. **The primary objective of an advertisement is to communicate its Propositional Benefit quickly, easily, fully, and memorably.** If everyone in advertising held fast and remained constant to that objective, we would never again see a magazine article titled "What the hell was *that* all about?"

Occasionally, you hear advertisers say that the objective of their advertising is to "excite the sales staff or trade" or to "sell in." But that's merchandising or promotion, not advertising used for its assigned role in the marketing process. OK, if that's how you want to use your budget, but don't expect the advertising to do much, if anything, for the product's Propositional Benefit—for its appeal to potential buyers or for brand equity.

Having said that advertising should work to make the Propositional Benefit known, I must add this: Advertising does not have exclusive rights to that job. Sometimes other routes may do it much better. Good and timely publicity, for example. The head-on collision of two Chrysler LeBarons, from which both drivers walked away unhurt, did much, much more than advertising could ever do for the proposition of "buy a Chrysler to enjoy the benefit of a driver-side airbag as standard equipment."

Similarly, the word-of-mouth that results from a product's performance or simply its appearance can work to spread a proposition more successfully than can advertising. Back when the first Mustang was introduced, I remember the agency boasting that it had done the most successful car-introduction advertising ever. I, and most others, considered the advertising routine (and it proved off-target at that, being aimed at the "youth market," when the average age of the Mustang buyer turned out to be about 49). All that long-and-low-hooded sporty beauty, selling for something under $3,000, had to do was appear in show rooms and on the highways, and it was an instant case of "I want *that!*"

None of this, however, takes away from the fact that advertising almost always does—or should do—the bulk of the work to make the Propositional Benefit quickly, easily, fully, and memorably clear.

The First Question

Whether or not enough people accept an advertisement's Propositional Benefit depends, of course, on the appeal of that benefit to them. You can judge the appeal of a proposition by asking a number of questions that all fall under the umbrella question, *"Where are people in relation to the product or category of product at this time?"* In other words, from that product or from that category of product, what do they want most at this time? For example, for many foods "at this time," people especially want low fat, no cholesterol, fewer calories, and low sodium. And that example dramatizes how "where people are" can change. Not long ago, if you said, "For lunch, I had a nice, creamy glass of milk, two eggs, some cheese, and bread and butter," everyone would have considered that a healthy lunch. Today, your friends would ask, "Are you trying to eat yourself to death?"

Companies do market research to try to determine where people are in relation to their product at any time. But don't underestimate your own human empathy for, your own experience with, your own exposure—and reactions—to other people. After you look at the printouts, look out the window. The smartest marketers use *both* research and their own human senses to develop a Propositional Benefit that appeals to the largest number of the right people, the people who might buy it. These marketers know that for a *product* to succeed, it *must* offer that benefit, whether real or perceived.

What about the Advertisement?   Simply because so many advertising people do *not* hold fast and remain constant to that primary objective, we see cases of the *product* offering an appealing benefit, but *not* the advertisement; the product proposition starts from where people are, *but the advertisement does not.*

Note carefully that word *start.* For an advertisement, the start means (1) its overall "look" (including color), (2) the major illustration (if any), or (3) the headline—whichever element is visually strongest. What people "read" into that element—if anything—*becomes* the offer of the advertisement, or the proposition, whether or not you intended it to be. So *if* that visually strongest element is not compatible with or helpful to your Propositional Benefit, the advertisement does not start from where people are, even if the product does. No use arguing, "But the benefit is in the copy." If people don't see it "at the start" or get good strong clues to it (or, as we will note in Chapter 4, if they don't see *some* benefit), they will never *get* to the copy.

Assuming the product positioning starts from where people are, in order to complete the "A" in the "A, B & C of Effective Advertising," you want an overall "look," a headline, and illustration which do the same. Then, whichever element people catch with an idle glance, the advertisement makes, or starts to make, the right proposition, the Right

Offer. What the first element seen *must not* do is make or start to make a "wrong offer."

Seeing It More Clearly Than Ever

I'm going to show you this principle of starting "where people are" at work—and not at work—in two different disciplines: *editorial* print and *advertising* print. This tactic has helped many people to see it, and other advertising principles and techniques, more clearly than ever before. I hope it does the same for you. Let's look first at some editorial examples, good and bad.

Over an article about a new, synthetic food with no calories, another magazine, not *Reader's Digest,* ran this title: **Food That Isn't Food**. Well, yes, people are always interested in food, but in that way? Do people dislike food so much that they want a nonfood food? Would they rather have a pill instead of a steak? No, of course not. People love to eat, don't they? But aren't they very much concerned "at this time" with the fattening ingredients of food? Isn't this the age of the calorie-counter? In *content,* the article under this headline appealed directly to that strong and current interest. In other words, the article contained the right Propositional Benefit. The *article* started from where people are, but the strongest visual element—in this case the headline—did not.

When the *Digest* condensed and ran the article, it carried the headline at right, which instantly and clearly starts from where people are.

New Food
That Can't Fatten You

Under an almost abstract—certainly weird-looking—rendering of a motorcycle, another publication ran the title **How Fermi Would Have Fixed It**. For two reasons, both related to the principle of starting where people are, that title and picture did not offer a strong Propositional Benefit for reading the article: First, very few people remember who Enrico Fermi was. (When conducting seminars, I always ask how many people in the audience *do* remember. The last time I did, out of over 100 in the audience, only 2 raised their hands.) Second, even if they did remember Fermi, people were puzzled by what they saw and read, or were not interested in how Fermi would have fixed a strange motorcycle, anyway. Enrico Fermi, however, did have an elegantly practical, logical—and learnable—method for solving all types of problems. Thus, when *Reader's Digest** condensed and ran the article, its editors illustrated and titled it this way:

Often, the titles in other publications are fine for *their* readers. For example, in a business publication, one which commonly carries stories about the workings of government agencies, the title page of an article had two visually strong elements: a picture of a group of men who appeared to be engineers or inspectors standing under the wing of an airplane, and a title reading **THE FAA'S LOOSE GRIP ON AIR SAFETY**. Fine for that magazine's readers. But for the *Digest*'s huge general audience of readers, its editors titled and illustrated a condensation of the same article as shown here.

*All *Reader's Digest* copyrighted editorial material reproduced with permission of Reader's Digest Association, Inc.

Sometimes, even though you start from where people are, you lack the intensity of interest that you could get by moving closer. To interest the greatest number of people, you try to get as *general* as possible. For greatest intensity of interest, you try to get more *specific*. These two actions work against each other. So it's a constant balancing act, with the question coming down to this: How specific can you get and still have a large audience?

One publication ran an illustration of a frowning little boy, arms folded and staring morosely out a window. A mother-like woman stood behind him, hands on her hips and a concerned expression on her face. Below this illustration was the title **TROUBLED KIDS**. This presentation wasn't bad. Anyone with a concern for children might see some interest there. The *Digest*, however, hit closer to home—and greatly increased the intensity of interest—with the title and illustration at right as its two strongest title-page elements.

How to Tell
When
Your Kids
Need Help

Caution when Applying the Principle Globally With the growing incidence of and interest in global advertising, it's worth noting this from the *Digest*'s experience with its worldwide network of editions: Almost always, the same product positioning that appeals to human beings in one country will appeal to human beings in other countries. But, to assure starting from where people are in each country, you must carefully watch your approach and wording (especially in translation).

Reader's Digest has editors in 23 countries editing in (as of 1992) 17 languages, and you can see this care in how they change titles when the same articles run in several countries. The U.S. editors once ran, for an article about British scientists coming to American laboratories, the title **Brains Across the Sea**. The British editors titled the same article **The Brain Drain**.

Over an article on fairy tales, the U.S. editors wrote, **Happily Ever After With the Brothers Grimm.** Our Spanish-writing editors made it **Y colorin colorado...** which actually means nothing—roughly, "That which is reddish is reddish." But to Latin American children, it means the end of the story...happily ever after.

There is no skill more valuable to editors—and to marketing and advertising people, as we shall see—than the skill of knowing where people are in relation to the sub-

ject you want to introduce, at the time you want to introduce it.

What interests them "now" because of what *else* is happening? That's easy. It was, for example, a no-brainer to know that, during the Persian Gulf War, millions of Americans who had never given that area a thought would suddenly become intensely interested in Middle East problems. Similarly, after an election for governor of Louisiana, the *Digest* started where readers were at that time by highlighting on its cover an article titled **DAVID DUKE: RACIAL POLITICS FOR PROFIT**. In journalism, they call that "using a news peg."

But a far greater, far more valuable, and far higher (hence more rare) skill demands truly sensitive empathy with *people as human beings*. Such empathy helps you know or sense what *always* interests people, no matter what else is happening. *Digest* editors rank as masters of this skill. Any issue will carry over a dozen titles illustrating this talent: **Ways to Boost Your Willpower, The Pig Who Loved People, What Kids Need Most in a Dad, How to Tell If Someone Is Lying, A Driving Tip to Save Your Life, How Experts Cope With Stress, Can You Handle a Medical Emergency?, How to Tell a Joke.** You can tack up the table of contents from any *Digest*, throw a dart, and hit a title as great for the same empathic reason.

The Critical Question   *Does it work in advertising, too?* Most emphatically, YES! Let's look at some pairs of advertising headlines to see what happens when they start from where people are—and what happens when they don't:

...take an Italian Airline to London?

Are you kidding?

Alitalia got a route from New York to London. The *simpatico* Italians understood, however, that anyone planning to fly between those two cities would *not* think first (if at all) about Alitalia. So they wrote a headline saying what you read at left.

Obviously, the Italians knew where Americans were at that time. But when you glanced at an advertisement for Cuisinart, you saw several Japanese-made food processors on one page, a Cuisinart by itself on the facing page, and a big, two-part headline over the Japanese and French products reading:

There are many food processors made in Japan. The original is still made in France.

Who *cares* if the original is still made in France? The French do, certainly, but the Americans at whom the advertisement aimed do not. Some Americans might believe that the original, Cuisinart, is the best; and if an advertisement claimed that, fine. But it gets no Brownie points simply by being made in France.

By the standard of starting from where most Americans are, especially women, we give a solid 10 to this headline: **Want to lose 4 pounds fast?** But suppose you asked someone the question of this headline: **Want a good reason to switch to Coffee Rich?** I can just hear that person responding, "No, I haven't been looking for one." At the bottom of that advertisement, under a large illustration of the product, were the words: **Here's 3: 1. Freshness 2. Taste 3. Savings.** Those words (despite the grammar) showed that the *marketing* people had done their job of developing a strongly appealing Propositional Benefit: Buy this product to enjoy the benefits of better taste, longer freshness, and lower cost. Again, the *product* started from where people are, but the *advertisement* did not.

Subtleties of Starting Where They Are   To always start from where people are, in every way, takes knowing or sensing a whole range of values and characteristics of people. Some of these traits are very subtle, but all seem fairly obvious once defined.

To illustrate, I'll give you an example chosen because it is one of those subtleties that get advertisers into trouble most often: In the lives of all those people out there, how important, or *un*important, is our product? Because we get so wrapped up in it, because our product means success or failure for us, *we* often present it as far more important than *they*, the consumers, see it. Read this headline for a laxative advertisement:

In today's environment even man could become an endangered species.

It seems to suggest that constipation could make man extinct! A bit overdone, wouldn't you say?

I think a German advertiser got the "scale of values" right with this advertisement (a translated and resketched facsimile):

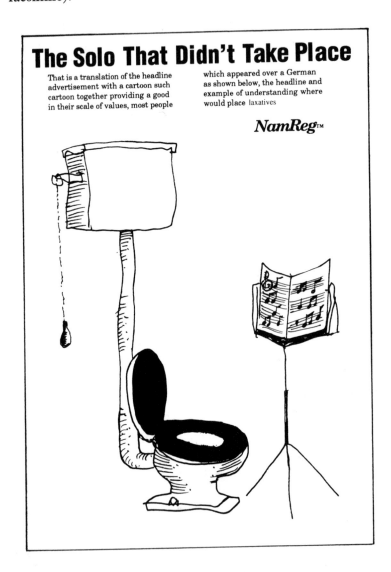

The Solo That Didn't Take Place

That is a translation of the headline advertisement with a cartoon such cartoon together providing a good in their scale of values, most people

which appeared over a German as shown below, the headline and example of understanding where would place laxatives

NamReg™

Watch for Land Mines   When you critique your advertisement for "where people are," use that sensitive empathy of yours to think of *everyone* who will see it. A copywriter for a product advertised to make gray hair shining silver tried to be clever by playing with an old saying: Over a picture of a vibrantly laughing older white woman, he or she wrote the headline, **Free, gray, and 51.** How carelessly insensitive to all the black women who remember and justifiably hate the original saying, **Free, white, and 21!** That's what I call putting your creative foot in your mouth—and, in Chapter 4, we'll see more results of the cleverness curse.

Watch Your Artwork, Too   Many times, your artwork will be the strongest visual element, hence the first one "read," in your advertisement. And that, too, should start from where people are. An advertisement showing a little girl washing her feet in a bidet worked fine in Europe. But in the United States, it brought the question, "Why is that kid washing her feet in the toilet bowl?"

Summary Time

The *A* in the A, B & C of Effective Print Advertising is the most *appealing* Propositional Benefit to the greatest number of the right people. You develop that proposition before you start to create any advertising, and you do it by, in every way, *starting from where people are in relation to the product at "this" time.* When you critique an advertisement, you ask the same question about it and about the visually strongest element in your advertisement, the one that will be seen first, and that must be compatible with and somehow helpful to your Propositional Benefit. If they are compatible, you can move on in your critique, as we can now move on to the *B* in the A, B & C of Effective Print Advertising.

The B: Quick, Easy Recognition of the Propositional Benefit

4

When readers come to your advertisement, they will give it only an idle glance. In that split second, possibly with their minds the proverbial million miles away, they must—I repeat, *must*—see or sense *some* reason to pause. The only thing that will make people pause is seeing or sensing something of interest—*some reward for pausing*.

If none of the visually strongest, thus first-seen, elements of your advertisement—in other words, neither the "look" of it, nor a major illustration, nor the headline, nor the key words—signal anything of interest to readers, they turn the page. And if that happens, then you might as well have not run the advertisement!

This make-or-break importance is why I call the instant your advertisement is first exposed to human eyes the *critical microsecond.* And why I consider it crucial to critique your advertisement by asking, "**Does a mere idle glance reveal *some* reason for anyone out there to pause?**" I emphasize the word *some* because if the signals that your advertisement emits, and that make people pause, can be signals of your Propositional Benefit, you're in clover. For then you can do what all great advertisements must do: *hit hard, fast, and home*. You can get right to communicating your proposition and go straight through communicating it.

But sometimes—nearly *all* the time for mature products—your proposition is no longer exclusive (if it ever was), or new, so a straight presentation of it no longer gives people reason to pause. That's when—although (and note this "although" carefully) you will *still end up communicating your proposition*—you may get people to pause with what I call a Laid-On Benefit. Not often, but *sometimes*, and very, very briefly, that can be an appeal other than your Propositional Benefit. We will expand on that later and explore Laid-On Benefits in Chapter 7.

Appeal to an *Existing* Interest

Whether you can start with your Propositional Benefit or must use a Laid-On Benefit, if you want people to pause with just an idle glance at your advertisement, you must appeal to an *already existing interest*. Even when—in fact, especially when—you have a new product to introduce, the key to success both in product positioning and in advertising is to relate to, and instantly signal that relationship to, a strong existing interest of people.

For years, I've made the following contention: After centuries of human existence, there really are no new interests, only new ways to satisfy existing interests. VCRs were new only a few years ago. Yes, but how old is the interest in entertainment? Microwave ovens—cooking in minutes, even seconds—they were new. But how old is the interest in the ability to cook fast when we want to? Our relatively newly discovered need for bran—for fiber—merely reflected old and continual interest in good health.

So follow this rule: If an advertisement, within the instant of an idle glance, signals something relating to an *existing* interest, it will get people to pause. If it does not, *they* will not.

In both Editorial and Advertising Sometimes, just the "look" of an article or an advertisement can signal a reason to pause. For example, suppose you were interested in religion, and you turned a *Reader's Digest* page and saw just the part of a title page at left.

The typography and the style of art (and if you could see it in color here, the purple) instantly signal that this article is about religion, that subject of interest to you.

Few people consider *Reader's Digest* to be a humor magazine, but humor is a fundamental ingredient of the globally read monthly. Among its most popular features, for example, are **Laughter**, **the Best Medicine**, **Humor in Uniform**, and **Campus Comedy**. It also runs many humorous articles. And the instant your eyes hit just the first part of this opening page, you see a reason to pause: a clear promise of humor.

The knowledge needed to signal "reason to pause" with just the "look" of your advertisement includes the touches that make the difference between an "active" and a "static" layout and the impressions given by different colors, by typography, and especially by different styles of art.

For its advertisement announcing new Kleenex® Softique®, Kimberly-Clark made some very sophisticated decisions about typography (to make it look ad hoc hand-lettered), layout (rebus-style), art style (sketches), and color (primarily pink) to create both an active "look" that aroused curiosity by "saying something interesting," and, at the same time, a feeling of "soft" (its Propositional Benefit).

With permission of Kimberly-Clark Corp.

Enter the Major Illustration

After readers get an initial impression from the overall "look" of an advertisement, their eyes invariably go to a major illustration (if any). Thus, that element, as much by its *style* (e.g., Softique's light sketches) as by its content, can do a large part of the job of signaling a reason to pause—as you have already seen, and as the following examples reinforce.

The instant your eyes see the two brooms sweeping, one so much better than the other, you are well on your way—from illustration alone—to understanding O'Cedar's proposition that its Angler gets the dirt that other brooms miss. And that understanding gives you a reason to pause if you ever sweep floors.

With permission of The Drackett Co.

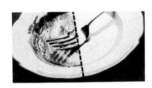

For the same reasons, I applaud Electrosol's major illustration. It not only helps communicate the Propositional Benefit but also gets people who wash dishes (the adult universe) to pause because they sense news of benefit for doing so.

I know that many in advertising would call these illustrations unimaginative Plain-Janes. I say Hurray! for the bona fide professionals who put clarity before cleverness, who know when not to even try to play games.

The so-called "creativity" that I deplore (but that often wins awards) puts cleverness before clarity. For example, an advertiser offered a good, tangible benefit: *frozen* grilled cheese sandwiches. To make a grilled cheese sandwich the "old-fashioned" way is quite a chore, and you end up with a sticky mess to clean. But to make a sandwich starting from frozen, you just put one in a toaster and, in minutes, up pops a beautiful grilled cheese sandwich. The "creative" people, however, couldn't leave this simple proposition alone. Playing on the headline word *American* grilled cheese sandwich, they painted stars and bars on the toaster.

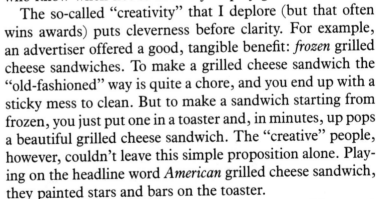

In seminars everywhere and for many years, I have put on the screen the whole advertisement containing this illustration. I have paused to take a drink of water, and then told the audience, "I deliberately left that on the screen while I paused to take a drink. I wanted to give you plenty of time. How many of you have yet seen the toaster?" *Never* has a hand immediately raised. Only after the audience searches the advertisement (which, remember, readers will *not* do) has one hand gone up . . . then another . . . then another. (I won't show you the whole advertisement because I don't want to put a mark on the reputation of one of the nation's most competent print advertisers. I leave the example in the script even when I do seminars in that company's head-quarters, where, confident of their record and abilities, they laugh as spontaneously as do audiences everywhere.)

What that bit of "cleverness" did was *camouflage the kitchen appliance that made the benefit possible!* I don't view that as clever, and neither have any audiences to which I have shown it. (But I can visualize it getting an advertising art award.)

Enter the Headline

Immediately after glancing at the major art—or simulta-neously, depending upon the juxtaposition of the art and headline—readers' eyes should catch at least the key words of the headline. These key words also can help greatly to sig-nal readers what they will get if they pause; and they will if the key words promise readers some benefit for their time.

Look at the headline at right over a *Digest* article. Sup-pose you were about to pay, had just paid, or someday would pay for a wedding and had heard friends bemoaning their purse-draining experience. Would the key words *High Price* and *Weddings* catch your eyes and pull you to that article?

**The
High Price
of
Weddings**

Key words are the ones that do the most to signal what the headline is about. If the topic interests you, they work like magnets, pulling you to them. The stronger the in-terest, the stronger the magnetic pull. (The strongest key-word magnet is your own name. If you glanced at your boss's desk and your name was on a piece of paper there, even upside down from where you stood, those "key words" would pull your eyes to them, you bet!) Consequently, it is very much worth paying attention to (1) getting meaningful key words into your headlines and (2) setting and stacking your headlines to make those key words easily seen with just a glimpse.

A good corporate advertiser has the great slogan at right that it used as the headline for an advertisement. This headline was fine for making that great slogan even bet-ter known than it is, and for the real value that widespread recognition brings to the company. But the headline car-ried no key words to signal that the advertisement contained

A Century of Caring

Arthritis:
Instead of alleviating
arthritic pain,
we could end up
eradicating it!

news of intense interest to a large number of people—news that added meaning to the slogan. Suppose, however, that the headline had been written, set, and stacked as shown at left. As a person with two arthritic knees, which make running impossible and even golf painful, I can testify that just the word *Arthritis* would pull me instantly to that headline. Followed by such words as *alleviating* and (oh, blessed day) *eradicating,* you could not keep me from reading that advertisement! (And I did not invent that headline, I took it verbatim out of the copy of the advertisement.)

(**Aside lesson:** This case teaches us something else, too. You want to make a slogan not only well known but also *meaningful.* Thus, it is always better to "give the reasons" and then *follow* with the slogan, as opposed to featuring the slogan first—which may be all people see—and then giving the reasons, which they may never read.)

Enter the Headline and Art Together

We have traced the path of the reader from the initial impression obtained from the "look" of an advertisement, to the impression from major art, to the impression from the key words of the headline. Remember, though, that all this happens in one or two ticks of a clock. Equally fast, we move to the *impression* from the headline and art *together.* (Still not consciously "reading.")

Choice Words
to Help You Choose

A magazine, not *Reader's Digest,* once ran the headline at left. Unless you're another editor noting the alliteration, you don't spot any words that catch your interest, do you? The artwork didn't help, showing as it did a seemingly puzzled woman standing at a fork in the path, with the fallen dot of a question mark rolling up one of the forks. For the same article, the *Digest* used the headline and illustration just below that. Instantly, you see the flipping quarter (heads or tails, you know what that means); and you catch the key words *help* and *hardest decisions.* Instantly, you see *several* clear signals of interest to you.

Help for
Your
Hardest   Decisions

Once again, I'm sensitive to the fact that you may think these points are elementary. But start looking critically at advertisements with this question in mind: Does anything you catch with just an idle glance signal *some* reason for you to pause? You will be surprised by how many advertisements have *not applied* principles that may seem elementary.

The Head-Swivel Test

The next time you are going to give a first look at a layout with art and headline in place, try what I call the "head-swivel test." Point your nose over your left shoulder and place the layout in front of you without looking at it. Now, with a fairly quick count of 1, 2, 3, swivel your head to look over your right shoulder, letting your eyes pass over the layout as your head turns. Did you catch anything meaningful? You *should*, or neither the "look" of the advertisement, nor the illustration, nor the headline worked as they must. That's all the time readers will give it. And remember, they are *not paying attention*!

As I write at this moment, I have an advertisement on my desk. I planned to include it here, but I haven't the heart. So to protect the guilty, I'll just describe it. You'll get the point. It's a spread, with the whole left page black except for a drum and a stroboscopically photographed hand holding a bass-drum stick and hitting down on the drum, apparently repeatedly. On the page facing this rather sterile illustration, the headline read as you see at right. I've always felt that headline should have read: **Now, now, now . . . is the time, time, time . . . to turn, turn, turn . . . the page, page, page**. I neither sensed nor saw any reason not to.

**Now, now now
...is the time, time, time.**

From "Pause" to "Stop"

Readers have turned a page, exposed your advertisement and given it an idle, mind-absent glance. During that microsecond, they have seen or sensed enough to make them pause. Now your advertisement has a chance turn that pause into a stop.

To do that, it must have two things:

1. A headline so easy to speed-read and understand that readers will have grasped it before they decide to try.
2. If you have a major illustration, one equally easy to "speed-read" and understand.

The "How-To" for Headlines Your headline will be easy to speed-read and understand if you follow the rule for all good *Digest* titles: **Use familiar combinations of words in familiar sequence**. This rule *does not* mean you should write in clichés. It means you should say it as close as possible to how "they"—all those people out there—would say it *in conversation*. Don't say it with that stilted "formality" so many slip into when writing, or equally bad if not worse, according to the cliché notion of how a big-league, slick advertisement should read.

Stilted language and adspeak slow down reading. Writing familiar combinations of words in familiar sequence always speeds it up. When such familiar language is used, even readers with no training in speed-reading will automatically apply one of the techniques of speed-reading: They will read not one word at a time, but several—four, five, or six—in what I call "visual gulps." Let's look at some examples of how this principle of familiarity makes for quicker, easier reading and understanding of headlines.

I have been partially deaf for most of my life. To bring my hearing to a level where I need wear only a tiny hearing aid, I have had two operations. At the conclusion of each operation, the surgeon has leaned over and asked me something, and I have replied. But I didn't say anything remotely like what was the title of an article about one of those operations; I didn't say anything about **Lifting the Curtain of Silence**. I said exactly what the *Digest* wrote for its title over the same article: **Doctor, I Can Hear!** You might be thinking, "that's so short no wonder it's easy to read." All right, let's look at some longer ones.

Another publication wrote and ran this rather school-bookish title: **The New Economics of Leasing**. But that's not how people talk. The *Digest* title over the same article, using familiar combinations of words, was: **Should You Lease Your Next Car?**

"A Pension for Trouble" in another magazine was not only an unfamiliar combination of words but also not understandable. (I wonder if they were trying to play cute with the word *penchant*?) The *Digest* title, a bit longer but completely conversational and certainly quicker reading and easily understandable, was: **How Bureaucrats Pad Their Pensions**.

Take David Ogilvy's advice. Look through—study—*Reader's Digest* titles. On page after page, you will find familiar combinations of words in familiar sequence, quick and easy to read and understand in visual gulps of several words at a time. In the examples below, a slash separates the visual gulps to show that although the titles range from five to eight words in length, they all contain just two visual gulps—they are essentially only two words:

When Your Health Insurer/Drives You Nuts
20 Ways to Save Money/at the Supermarket

When Should You/Trade In Your Car?
Give Voters/A Real Choice
Where Great Movies/Come From

The Same for Advertising The principle of familiar combinations of words in familiar sequence works in advertising, too. Under an appetite-appealing illustration of hot soup in a colorful soup mug, Campbell's Soup, that venerable print advertiser, ran this quick and easy to read 14-word headline—ordinarily considered too many words for an advertisement headline, but not when you write familiar words in familiar sequence, so that people read it in visual gulps—three, or four at the most for this head.

> The difference between
> a cold sandwich and a hot lunch
> is about five minutes.

For Gaines Puppy Choice® and with a heart-tugging photograph of a soft golden retriever puppy ran another otherwise long headline. This one contains 13 words, but only three visual gulps.

> **Would you feed
> a soft little puppy like this
> something hard and dry?**

How about a headline of 39 words plus 3 numbers? In familiar combinations of words in familiar sequence, look at how fast it reads:

> **To the thousands of people who've
> tried to call for reservations on the
> Auto-Train™ and gotten a busy signal:**
>
> **1. We've doubled our phones.**
> **2. We've added many more agents.**
> **3. And we're now taking your calls
>   seven days a week.**

Could you possibly write it any more conversationally? I count it as only eight—nine at the most—visual gulps, and I'll wager you read it all in under ten seconds (I just now timed it again). Great job!

From now on, don't let anyone tell you that "there are too many words in that headline." As you have just experienced for yourself, it's not the number of *words* that determine how fast and easily you can read and understand a headline. It's the *familiarity* of the words and the sequence, and the number of visual gulps it takes to "gulp" through it, several words at a time.

When you don't "say it the way they would say it"—that is, as you would in conversation—people have to read one word at a time. This point leads to an interesting test: If you can't say a headline fast and easily, chances are it won't read that way, either. Try saying this aloud and fast:

> **calms, quiets
> nagging coughs fast**

I'm always asked if using familiar combinations of words excuses incorrect grammar if that's "the way they would say it." The answer is yes and no. Yes, if it has become common (and accepted) English usage. That old English-teacher brouhaha over "Winston tastes good like a cigarette should" was nonsense because we commonly use the word *like* for *as*. But the headline at left gets a "NO!"

There's two sides to every story

Playing with Words   I'm asked also if using familiar language means just writing "plain English," never playing around with words, never doing "something different," never getting any zip and/or FUN into a headline. Well, plain English is not a bad idea—it's better than adspeak. But, *if* while you're working to be clear, something delightful comes to you—and it does not detract from clarity—I say with all possible enthusiasm: GO FOR IT!

The *Digest* "plays with words" for many of its best titles. Look at these two examples:

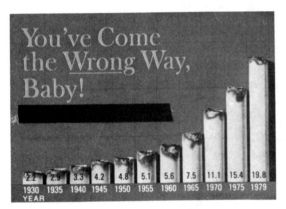

The *Digest's* British editors do a marvelously witty job using puns to create headlines with fun in them, as with the egg example at left.

U.S editors join in with puns of their own: After we lost the America's Cup to Australia, they ran an article lamenting:

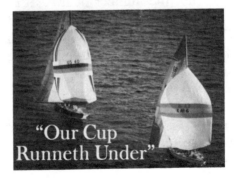

Again, the Same for Advertising In advertising, too, you certainly can play with words to write and run headlines with delightful twists, headlines that instantly put an impactive new perspective on a proposition or that are just plain fun! Most often, the "play-with-words" headline works best when you don't really have anything new or exclusive or in any other way extraordinary to say. You have a perfectly good proposition, but just a straight statement of it won't have much punch. Or, in some cases, a straight statement would get you to the level of EFFECTIVE, but a more dramatic, more colorful, more demonstrative way to say it might move you to the level of GREAT.

For its Japanese-made Colt, with the proposition being low sticker price, Chrysler could have simply put the price in the headline. It *did* show the price large and bold in the copy area, but it gave the proposition an extra something with the headline at right.

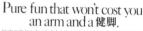

With permission of Chrysler Corp.

Hanes could have said that its socks might cost more than other socks, but they had reinforced toes to make them wear longer. Such an advertisement would have been EFFECTIVE. But Hanes moved toward greatness with this headline and illustration:

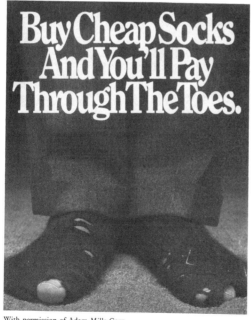

With permission of Adam Mills Corp.

Notice—*study, learn,* and *remember*—that those plays on words *do* state the proposition. I can't emphasize that point too strongly. Plays on words, or any other cleverness, that do nothing for the proposition may entertain but don't help sell. If you can sell by entertaining, bravo! But so many people in advertising need to learn and hold to the conviction that we're *marketers*—sales people—*not* entertainers!

Dangers in Cleverness Another reason to beware of cleverness is that it's terribly difficult to *be* clever, and so easy to end up with our creative feet in our mouths, as did, in my mind, whoever wrote **THE SPORTS SEDAN FOR PEOPLE WHO INHERITED BRAINS INSTEAD OF WEALTH.** I'm sure all the people who have inherited wealth don't feel that they were shortchanged on brains.

A pervasive and boomeranging form of attempted cleverness these days has copywriters playing with old expressions while apparently not understanding the nuances of their meanings. For the United Way, with a picture of people standing knee-deep in flood water, I saw a headline saying **Some people have had the United Way up to here.** Another showed an old man eating, with the headline **Some people get fed up with the United Way.** The series included others in which so-called cleverness was supposed to promote but, instead, ended up bad-mouthing the United Way.

So I repeat, go for it; but be careful—and you better be good.

A Brief Note on Typography Brief not because it's unimportant. In print advertising, typography is, in fact, so critically important I have devoted a chapter (10) to it. But I would leave out an absolutely necessary part of this section if I did not say this: We can write a headline that, in wording, is wonderfully easy to scan-read and comprehend—one also with several interest-grabbing key words. But also we can (and, unfortunately, we too often do) with bad typography (i.e., poor typeface, bad leading, illogical line breaks) make it nearly impossible to grasp easily and rapidly, or even to see the key words. You will read and see how in Chapter 10.

Easily Understood Art Just as the headline must be so easy to read that people read it before they consciously decide to, the illustration must be so easy to "read" and understand that people instantly know what it "says." And the rule for illustrations is very much like the one for headlines: **Use familiar objects in familiar patterns.** (Now, you art directors, calm down! This does not mean plain, simple, or unimaginative, as I will demonstrate.)

You can use familiar objects in a familiar pattern and make them much more than ordinary by your treatment of them, as in this piece of *Digest* art, which drops the half-tone out of the bodies to emphasize the tenderness of the mother's face next to the child's.

You can use familiar objects in a somewhat unfamiliar pattern as long as people immediately understand it. For example, jigsaw puzzle pieces, guns, and the Arabic star and crescent are familiar objects. Thus, when the *Digest* used them for an imaginative piece of art to lead off this article, it used familiar objects in a different way to say "putting the pieces together."

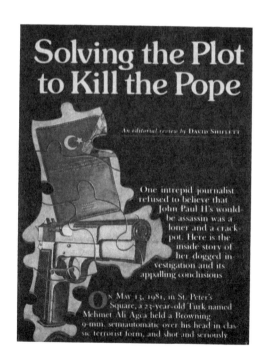

And Again, the Same for Advertising As with everything else, the same critical requirement applies to an advertising illustration: People must understand it the instant they see it. You can "play" with the art just as long as the playing does not detract from quick easy understanding.

If, for jams and jellies, you must make the *not*-exclusive proposition of natural ingredients, you can put fresh strawberries on a slice of bread, with the right headline, to greatly dramatize *your* claim, as Breyers™ did:

We're this natural, but easier to spread.

Breyer's is a registered trademark of Kraft General Foods. Reproduced with permission.

To dramatize the proposition that a ski watch tells not only the time but also the temperature, you can show the watch on a skier's arm in a block of ice:

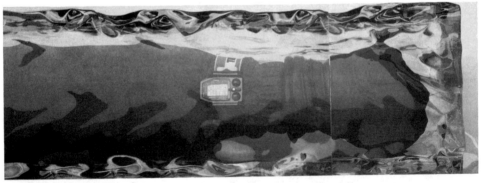

Reproduced with permission of Timex Corp.

In a series of advertisements for its Skiathlom® watch, Timex brilliantly dramatized also that it fit over the outside of a parka sleeve by illustrating it on a bear's paw, and that it was hard to break by showing it on an arm in a plaster cast, the watch being over the cast. A truly great series!

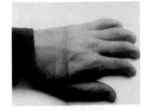

But a later advertisement in the series demonstrated a caution we must all heed—be careful when you are trying to be clever (and especially when you seem to be on a roll, because that's when you are most vulnerable to going too far). To illustrate that a ski watch should be easy to operate, they ran this all-thumbs illustration.

To every audience that has seen it, this illustration has come off as grotesque, deformed, puzzling, and not at all funny. (We shouldn't be too harsh. After all, with the four advertisements I saw, Timex batted .750, which, in baseball, is astounding.)

A creative director once challenged me, "Tony, if we don't use new forms of art expression, where are people ever going to learn what they mean?"

"Well," I replied, "probably in art galleries. You're not paid to teach people new forms of art expression. Your job is to use familiar forms of art expression, including with imagination, to communicate quickly, easily, clearly. Why, if we used your logic in copy, we could say that Americans are notorious for having only one language. So why don't we, here in the States, run the copy in, say, German. Eventually, some people might learn how to ask, 'Wie geht es Ihnen?' . . . but you wouldn't have the account, if it was still in business."

I've heard the argument that "people don't have to understand, that you can make them pause, even stop, by intriguing—by puzzling—them." This, to me, completely misunderstands the act of being intrigued. You are never intrigued by *nothing*. Surely people were intrigued by the first Timex illustration, but they immediately understood that an arm wearing a watch was inside a block of ice. They were intrigued to know *why* it was there, not *what* it was. I repeat, if you understand nothing you cannot possibly be intrigued. American men surely would be intrigued by the title **Ten Signs of Early Impotency**, but not if it were printed in Chinese!

Summary Time

In the A, B & C of Effective Print Advertising, the "B" is making some *benefit* instantly apparent to readers. At first, by seeing or sensing some reason to *pause* (hopefully a hint of the Propositional Benefit, but, as I promised to explain later, for a flash instant it can be anything readers view as a reason for pausing). Immediately after, we want readers to see a specific reason to stop.

We try for the "pause" with:

1. The "look" of our advertisement
2. And/or the style and/or the content of our major illustration (if any)
3. And/or key words of our headline

We try for the "stop" with:

1. A headline so easy to speed-read that people read it before they decide to
2. An illustration (if any) equally quick and easy to understand

And *we* understand that none of this keeps us from using all the imagination we have.

The C:
The Propositional Benefit Made Fully Clear

5

N ow we have our readers stopped because they recognize that the advertisement will make a proposition of interest to them. To keep them long enough to deliver our entire proposition, we must do one more thing for them: **Make it easy for them to move through the advertisement and, in so doing, understand the Propositional Benefit quickly and fully.**

Yes, of course, some Propositional Benefits have no details to make clear. An illustration and a headline, a meaningful slogan, or simply the style or flavor of the creative execution may do it all (e.g., many cigarette, soft drink, beer, and liquor advertisements). But most advertisements must say more than that.

Index of Comprehension

Study this Index for a moment, then continue reading.

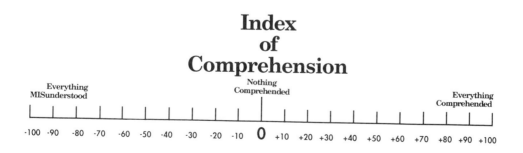

When readers are on 0, they comprehend—understand—nothing. They haven't the foggiest notion of what an advertisement will propose; they may not yet even be aware of the advertisement. The farther the advertisement moves them off 0 toward plus 100, the more of the proposition they understand. If, in the time readers will give, the advertisement can move them all the way to plus 100, hallelujah! that's the goal! But always remember that readers will *not work* to get to that plus 100 mark. It's entirely up to the advertisement—to you—to pull them, lure them, and cajole them there. You must make it worth their while to keep going toward plus 100.

In critiquing an advertisement for the "C," we must go back and reexamine some of the same elements we have already checked, but now for *different* purposes. In the "A" we were looking for the strongest possible benefit to the largest number of people. In the "B" we analyzed what, if anything, the "look" of the advertisement, key words of headline, the headline in full, and/or the illustration did to help make people pause; and then what, if anything, the headline and the illustration did to make them stop. Now, in the "C," we examine some of these same elements for their contribution toward *making the Propositional Benefit quickly, easily and fully clear.*

Idle Glancing Again

Remember, from earlier on, we wanted to know if just idle glancing revealed *some* reason to pause? Now we want to know if that *some* reason was the *right* reason. We want to know if that reason helps move people off 0 toward plus 100 or if an idle glance leaves them on zero.

THE WAR BETWEEN THE GENERATIONS

An article in one publication carried the headline at left. Which generations? What are they fighting about? Music? Haircuts? Clothes? That headline leaves you pretty much on 0.

Social Security: Will You Get Yours?

The article dealt with the specific and very serious problem of working generations paying for Social Security and retired generations receiving it. The *Digest* titled its condensation as you see at left. That certainly moved readers off zero, and in the *right* direction.

As Always, the Same in Advertising When my eyes first fell on the visually strongest elements of this advertisement, I didn't budge off 0. Neither did my wife. (And what a shame because the marketing people at the client certainly developed a fine proposition of yogurt in a pop-up can, needing no refrigeration, thus making it great for kid's lunch boxes.)

Leaving people on zero is bad enough. Worse yet is moving them off zero in the *wrong* direction. I remember a series of very good advertisements giving health hints— very good in what they said. But *au courant* among art directors at that time was a layout style that looked like a circus poster, and these advertisements followed that clownish fad. As a result, although the sponsor wanted to talk about health, the first impression said "humor." When I was invited to comment on the advertisement, I asked, "What would you do if, while a doctor gave you advice, he giggled? Your serious health hints are giggling." The layout sent people off 0 in the wrong direction.

In another magazine, *Digest* editors found an article titled as you see at right. With that headline, the article carried a picture of an Elizabethan-costumed man with a dash-line around his neck. That, together with the mystery-novel word *whodunit*, gave the quick impression that the

History's Biggest Literary Whodunit

Who Wrote Shakespeare?

article reported on who cut off the man's head. However, the article was actually about a fairly widely asked, much debated question, which led the *Digest* to use the headline you see at left. Now you speed off zero in the *right* direction toward plus 100—and with just a quick glance.

As previously noted, readers' eyes will invariably go first to illustrations, usually to the illustration at the *top* of a page. So, upon turning a page and revealing the next advertisement, your eyes would see this art and probably catch at least the first part of this headline:

Alas, poor Adult Nut,
you have but little chance
of ever going to a party.

What would be your first impression? I thought it was a headache remedy advertisement. But, no, that sends us off in the wrong direction. The advertisement's product actually was edible party nuts.

Take a quick look at this illustration:

That lovely Norman Rockwellish photograph gets high marks for its artistry—it might make some women pause nostalgically (possibly a few men, as well). But which way would they be heading off zero? Toward a proposition to buy and use what? Would you have ever guessed a certain brand of water faucet? That's what the advertisement proposed you buy.

When, during seminars, I put onto the screen an advertisement with this illustration, I say, "You see the mother and the baby, and the arrow going from the camera to the baby and back. Instantly, you know it's about a camera that does something automatically." (When someone once called out, "Yeah, it shoots kids!" that convulsed the audience and me, but it did not detract from the fact that the illustration does, indeed, move you off zero in the right direction.)

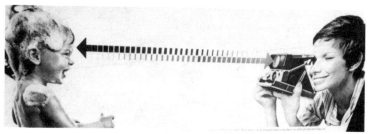

With permission of Polaroid Corp.

The Headline Again

Next in the C, we scrutinize the headline once more, again for a different purpose than earlier. Now we want to know this: Does the headline *help to communicate the Propositional Benefit*; or, if not, does it *orient* readers to receive it quickly and easily via the subhead, copy, and/or illustration?

Another magazine ran an article about a problem that vexes most everyone and seems to be getting worse. The article carried the title **WAS MAN MEANT TO FLY?** You know the facetious answer to that familiar question: If man was so meant, what God would have given him? If the article had been about man as *pilot*, that title might have at least oriented you to what you might get from reading it. But the article was *not* about man as pilot, but rather, about man as *passenger*—harried, hassled, delayed, and stranded by canceled flights. The *Digest* titled its version **Beating the Air-Travel Blues**. Now we know that we might get some useful information to help make our air travel more trouble-free. And the headline started you toward receiving that benefit.

Another title in another magazine read **A PENNY FOR YOUR THOUGHTS.** I didn't know what to make of that. In content, the article offered a chance to compare your compensation with people in many other kinds of jobs. That made the *Digest* change the title to **How Good Is Your Salary?** This title contributed toward moving you off zero, toward getting the benefit offered by the article.

Do the Same in Advertising I don't think it unfair to say that this headline leaves you sitting like one of those duck decoys—right on zero going nowhere:

IF you stayed with the advertisement long enough, you would have learned that the proposition was to buy a new issue of postage stamps that pictured beautiful duck decoys and honored folk art (then you also would have understood the play on "crafty"—arts and crafts, get it?). For people who collect stamps, this advertisement made an attractive proposition, but the headline did nothing to start to tell them about it.

A deliciously appetite-appealing advertisement for a smoked sausage carried this headline at top: **Discover The Missing Link**. I can imagine the client plaintively asking, "I know you people are the advertising experts, but can't we work the sales point in *some*where?" And the "creatives" grudgingly adding, in smaller type and at the bottom: **Finally, a Great-Tasting Smoked Sausage That's 90% Fat Free**.

Thank heaven some people in advertising know a fine proposition when they see one; and they know better than to play with it. I mean the good, professional people who write headlines such as this:

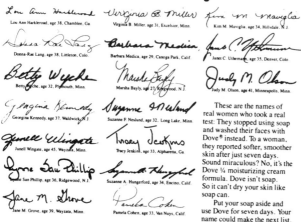

The headline makes clear what the Propositional Benefit is, and just the sight of the signatures adds to the meaning of the headline.

If you and your spouse want fervently to have a baby, you don't need words any fancier than those at right to reveal the benefit of reading the advertisement under it.

How to have a baby when you want to.

See how simple—and simply great—it is when the headline gets right to work to either start communicating the propositional benefit or to orient people so they are ready to get—easily, fully, and quickly—what the rest of the advertisement offers.

Illustrations Must Help

In this job of moving readers off zero to as close as you can get them to plus 100 (i.e., making the Propositional Benefit quickly, easily, and fully clear), illustrations can make a major contribution (either alone or, as we will note in the next section, in combination with the headline). In fact, if an illustration does not make some significant contribution, it's a waste of space. So, in our element-by-element critique for the "C," next we want to know *if the illustration helps to communicate the Propositional Benefit*; or, if not that, does it *orient* people to receive the benefit quickly, easily, and fully from the rest of the advertisement?

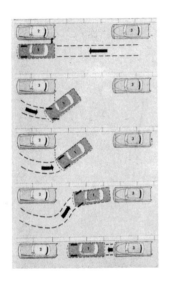

For an example of how the art alone can work in this job of getting readers off 0 and moving in the right direction toward understanding (even receiving) the Propositional Benefit, look at the drawing at left from a *Reader's Digest* article.

From the art alone, what do you think this article proposed to help you learn how to do? In fact, what benefit did the artwork, itself, actually *start to deliver?* Of course.

I know, only because I *studied* the advertisement, that the above illustration was meant to play off a headline saying that an improved chocolate chip cookie is "almost out of this world." But the sight of what seemed to be a meteor-battered planet neither moved me toward understanding the Propositional Benefit nor prepared me to understand it. Rather, it sent me off in another direction, toward *minus* 100, thinking that this was something about outer space.

By contrast, from seeing just the illustration of an advertisement for Knox Gelatine, what do you think Knox Gelatine proposed to do for your house plants? Of course.

*3 Applications

Headline and Art
Must Work Together

After checking the headline and illustration *separately* for the "C" (making the Propositional Benefit easy to understand quickly and fully), we continue the critique by asking: *Do the headline and major art help each other* (1) by both "saying" the same thing, (2) by the headline making the art more clear, or (3) by the art making the headline more clear?

The *Digest* rarely uses art for decoration. It uses art attractively but in a functional way, as part of the communication process. Most often, *Digest* art works with the title (1) to start to make clear the benefit offered by the article, and/or (2) to actually start delivering the benefit, and/or (3) to thoroughly orient readers to receive the benefit quickly and easily. This piece on the James Coco diet is a great example:

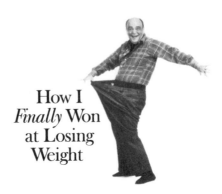

When you make a headline and illustration work together, it's like adding hand movements and facial expressions to spoken words. You make the two strongest elements in your layout stronger still, and you create a "communicating unit" more powerful than either one alone.

In Advertising When you make these two elements work together, you do something great or at least very good. When you overlook making them work together, or *don't* do it right, you waste a valuable opportunity. You slow down or do nothing for—or even do something counterproductive to—the movement toward plus 100.

What do you suppose was the Propositional Benefit, judging from the simulated illustration under this headline?

The breakthrough — the Propositional Benefit: An airline had configured its 747B's to offer "six adult-size Slumberettes, each with warm blankets and soft pillows." But, instead of showing you what a Slumberette looks like, or possibly a cross-section of the first-class cabin showing where and how six adults could sleep in what I assume are bed-like arrangements, they showed you a man's tonsils, which were not very attractive, and *certainly not very informative.*

If you own and love a Bernina (as does my wife), the name alone might attract your interest to this advertisement. But the headline and art together certainly don't do anything toward helping you understand the Propositional Benefit:

I, at first, thought it would propose that sewing with such a fine machine is relaxing. Actually, the benefit is that the machine automatically adjusts thread tension for different materials. But no help in understanding that benefit came from the headline and the illustration, either separately OR together.

The headline and illustration for the Hilton Supp-hose advertisement on the next page provide an excellent demonstration of head and art working together to not only introduce the Propositional Benefit but also to actually (and dramatically and memorably) deliver it. This great advertisement hardly needed any copy.

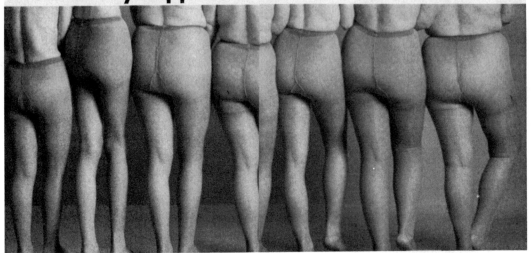

This is why Supp-hose comes in seven sizes.

Have you ever tried to put a pat of butter on a hot cob of corn? Does that familiar experience make this headline and illustration the work of clear-headed, 100% professional craftsmen? Yes, sir! If people gave that advertisement time only for the headline and illustrations, they *got it all*—quickly, easily, fully, and memorably. Reading the copy (short and nicely set) was a bonus.

Parkay is a registered trademark of Kraft General Foods. Reproduced with permission.

I couldn't believe my ears when a "big-time" creative director asked me (and in obvious exasperation), "Tony, what the hell do you want to do, give it all away with the head and the art?" And I don't think he could believe *his* ears when I replied (enthusiastically), "Hey, can you do that? I would love and approve it instantly!" *He* believed that, with the headline and illustration, you should lure people in, then *require* them to read the copy to understand the proposition. He *said* that. And I replied, "Unless you can be there every time your advertisement gets exposed—and with a gun—good luck on *forcing* people to read advertising copy."

And Last, Brevity

In Chapter 9, we will study how to condense copy, to make it no longer than it needs to be. For this chapter, it's enough to note that brevity is essential in advertising, but also that brevity *is a relative measure*. In your company magazine, a short item about someone else's accomplishments may be too long for you. An item about you, however, can't be long enough.

After a seminar in Puerto Rico, a copywriter asked, "Mr. Antin, do you know why I love to write ads for *Reader's Digest*? Because it's a *reading* magazine, and I can write long copy to get everything in." He was such a nice person that I hated to disagree, but I had to respond truthfully, "If a magazine which has as the keystone of its success the word *condensation* encourages you to write long copy, that's a paradox."

"Well, then," the copywriter asked, "what is just the right length? How long can the copy be?"

Being Italian and talking to Latinos, I responded, "How long should you make love? As long as you continue to interest the other party, keep going. When you no longer can, you must stop."

You're too old to wear Ruth Scharf?

Pity.

With permission of Ruth Scharf, Ltd.

To the people at whom a Ruth Scharf advertisement was aimed, these few words said all that needed to be said. So when they said only that much, that was brevity.

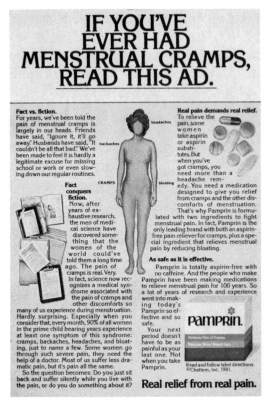

With permission of Chattem, Inc.

If you have quite a bit to say and it is all interesting to certain readers (as the above certainly was to women who suffer cramps), and if the copy moves right along, then two full columns *also* qualify as brevity.

How do you judge if copy "is all interesting to certain readers?" Note that this is a different question from how do you say as much in fewer words. Because making uninteresting copy shorter does not make it interesting. But recognizing what is uninteresting greatly helps in keeping copy brief because it reveals what to cut. Here are some of the most common causes of uninteresting sentences and paragraphs in advertising copy:

1. Running a block of copy when you don't need one at all. The headline and major illustration leave nothing more of interest to say.

2. Starting the copy with what people already know very well, or with what they don't care about (e.g., "When you have a splitting headache, you can't think of anything else." *I know! What have you got for my splitting headache?*)

3. Repeating the headline or the content of it in the first sentence. (Yes, I know that, in advertising, some repetition can sometimes help.)

4. Doing the same—repeating the headline—at the end of the copy.

5. Having so much fun playing with words that you can't resist putting in another and another "grace note" (e.g., in a toothpaste advertisement, after the copy claimed that more people use it than any other toothpaste, adding, "*And that sure makes the world a nicer place for teeth.*" After claiming that for tartar control it beats regular toothpaste by 44%, adding, "*Any way you look at it, there's just no contest.*" [How do you spell the sound of a yawn?]).

6. Not stopping when you have nothing more to say (e.g., "*You'll be glad you did.*").

My work at the *Digest* gave me another unique opportunity to learn—to learn how to condense advertising copy from some 30 years of doing it in my *Digest*-bred and advertising devotion to brevity. I applied what I had learned about condensing from *Digest* editors, plus a few techniques special to advertising copy—techniques I developed to accommodate marketing and legal requirements (and also egos). You will find what I learned, and what you can learn, in Chapter 9.

Summary Time

In critiquing for the C in the A, B & C of Effective Print Advertising, we start by visualizing the Index of Comprehension, and by asking a question we asked in the B, only now for a different reason: Does an idle glance at our advertisement reveal *some* reason to pause or possibly stop? Now, in the C, we ask if it is the—or a—*right* reason. Does what readers *first* see and comprehend (the "look" of the advertisement, key words of the headline, the headline itself, and/or the illustration) move them off 0 and toward plus 100 (i.e., toward total understanding of the Propositional Benefit)?

Next, we ask if the headline kicks in to start delivering the Propositional Benefit, or, at least, says something that makes getting it from the other elements of the advertisement quick and easy? And what about the major illustration (if any)? Does it help move people still farther along the line toward plus 100?

Continuing the critique for the C, do the headline and major illustration work *together* to make the combination stronger in communicating power than either element alone?

Finally, is the copy brief relative to the value of the benefit to "all those people out there"? A question we ask with the understanding that brevity can be a few words or many.

When we have finished critiquing for the A, the B, and the C, we have answers to the questions:

A: Does the advertisement offer the strongest possible Propositional Benefit to the largest possible number of the right people?

B: Do all the elements of the advertisement work to make it quick and easy for people to understand what Propositional Benefit is being offered?

C: Do all the elements of the advertisement work to make it easy for people to understand that Propositional Benefit quickly, clearly, and fully?

And, if we have confident "yes" answers to the A, the B and the C, we have Effective Print Advertising. Now, starting with the next chapter, we get into the major parts of what we do to reach that level *all* the time.

PART TWO

Executing
the A, B & C
of Effective
Print
Advertising

Layout:
So Elementary
But
So Surprisingly
Misunderstood

6

L ayout plays an essential role in executing the "B" and the "C." And it's mostly so elementary that I risk insulting the intelligence of mature professionals reading this book. But, astoundingly, layout also is so widely misunderstood that I *must* include it.

Not only college students, but also many working in advertising would list as the primary objectives of layout (1) making the advertisement beautiful (or startling or somehow "different") and (2) giving it flavor. I accept both as *sometime* objectives but not as THE primary, never-to-be overlooked objectives.

The Two Primary
Objectives of Layout

They are:

1. To assure that idly glancing eyes will see or sense the parts of an advertisement that signal some benefit for pausing. By their position and treatment to make those parts the visually strongest elements in the advertisement.

2. To give readers who have thus been pulled to a pause and stop:

- The *impression* that it will be quick and easy to understand fully the Propositional Benefit for which they stopped.
- The *experience* that it actually *is* quick and easy. It must not only *look* easy, it must actually *be* easy, or they will stop trying the instant they feel it more bother than it's worth to them.

To Make "Benefit Signals" Visually Strong

As I have already noted in Chapter 4, sometimes just the overall "look" of an advertisement will signal *some* benefit, *some* reason to pause. But, although layout has some effect, that overall "look" comes not so much from layout as from illustration style and content, typography, and color. Where layout can make a big difference in getting readers to pause is in causing key words of the headline (or the *whole* of a very short headline) and key illustrations to *stand out*.

To make key words in a headline stand out, to so handle them that even the most indifferent glimpse might cause them to register:

1. Set the whole headline large and bold in relation to the "environment" (i.e., the dimensions of the advertisement and of the publication). What's "large and bold"? Well, use your artistic sense of proportion to decide what size and weight would seem "right" in relation to the other elements. Then, if possible, go bolder, and definitely go up about 10–15% in point size. Yes, that's right: Make it bigger and bolder than you originally planned—actually "over-sized."
2. Put key words at the beginnings and ends of lines, not in the middle. If you break and stack the headline into more than two lines, write to permit putting key words at the beginnings and/or ends of the first and last lines.

Instead of: **If trading in your car is in your plans, lower rates make this the right time to do it.**

Try to do this: **If you plan to trade in your car, this is the right time to get lower rates.**

3. Use Dynamic Headlining—a headline concept that I describe and illustrate fully in Chapter 10 and that, as one of its advantages, breaks and stacks lines specifically to make key words stand out like this:

If you plan to trade in your car, this is the right time to get lower rates.

Pictures Top, Sometimes Left Given the size of a typical magazine page, it really does not matter where you place key illustrations—eyes will go there first. (Though that might be the *wrong* place for the right flow through the advertisement, as we will discuss just below.) But visualize a full-size newspaper spread. A reader could, with a glance at the upper left quarter, for example, not even see the rest of the advertisement; going from that quarter to the lower right quarter demands a movement not only of pupils but also of head. For a full-spread newspaper advertisement, I suggest positioning any benefit-signaling illustration "above the fold" and, unless it runs completely across a section center-spread, to the left.

Keep Head and Art Together To make your headline and illustration work together for strongly signaled benefit, especially on a full newspaper page or spread, put them together in the layout. I have heard and read some research-backed and just plain opinion-backed advice about whether headlines should be placed *over* or *under* pictures. *Under* seems to be the most advised. And when you want to make maximum use of your square inches, *do* put the picture above the headline so you can use the bleed space. But except in an unlikely case of a humongous headline and a blah picture, eyes will always go to the illustration first, so I don't think it much matters. Put the headline *alongside* an illustration if that makes the most sense. Just remember: If they must *work* together, *keep* them together.

To Make the Proposition Easy to Follow

For readers to follow your proposition easily, their eyes must *enter* the advertisement where they should (where the proposition starts to unfold), *track through* the advertisement (easily and as they *should* track to absorb the proposition), and *exit* the advertisement where they should. For this sequence, layout makes *all* the difference.

A number of people have researched this, and, with gratitude, I will cite one authority's findings. I will tell you in advance, though, that the research confirms what you already know (or should know) about people—in this case about how they read.

You know we read a page from the upper left corner to the lower right corner, in a series of horizontal sweeps, always moving *down* from where we start. (The research term is "reading gravity.") And, if the page has, let's say, three columns of copy, we read down the first (left) column, shoot up to the top and read down the second, and do the same for the third. We have been trained to read in that pattern, feel most comfortable doing it, and, thus, find it easiest to read that way.

Accommodate Readers If you simply accommodate what people find easiest to do, you can't go wrong. But if you ignore this human conditioning, that's another form of not starting from where people are, and you surely *can* go wrong.

Australian typography expert Colin Wheildon studied the way people scan printed pages. His findings:

	Comprehension Level		
	Good	Fair	Poor
Layouts complying (accommodating how people normally read)	67%	19%	14%
Layouts disregarding (how people normally read)	32%	30%	38%

Published by Newspaper Advertising Bureau of Australia, Ltd.

In a bountifully informative treatise (dealing primarily with newspaper-size advertisements but containing much that applies to print advertisement in any publication), Wheildon showed a "for instance" newspaper advertisement that ignores "reading gravity" (i.e., the fact that once started at a certain level, eyes don't easily move up and especially don't move to the *left* and up).

In this case, Wheildon's studies showed that eyes went first to the illustration at top center, then to the headline below it, then down the second column just below the headline, and then up to and down the third and fourth columns. People were not likely to read the column starting above and to the left of the illustration even though (to give the layout every chance) Wheildon put a large, bold initial letter at the top of that column.

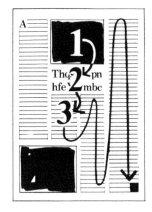

Actually, although it perfectly illustrates trying to defy "reading gravity," Wheildon's layout is only mildly bad. I can show you layout jungles into which you would not want to go without a tetanus shot. Believe it or not, one such advertisement expected you to track through it like this (and if you find it a maze, even with the numbers to help you, that's the point):

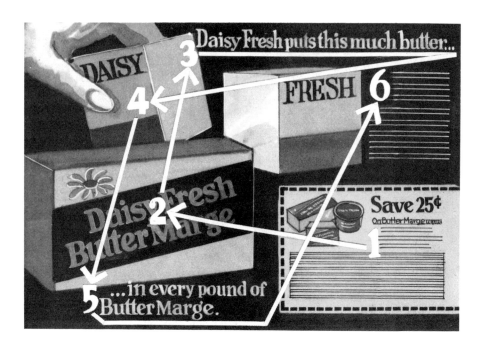

You can never be faulted for doing a layout with picture at top, followed by headline, followed by copy through to logo. And no reader will consider it boring. Good layout, like good typography, goes essentially unnoticed. Bad layout risks going unread.

Of course I don't mean you must—or even should—always use that classic layout. To prime your creative pump,

I asked a fine art director, Tony Mancino, to diagram four *different* layouts, all obeying the rules for easy tracking:

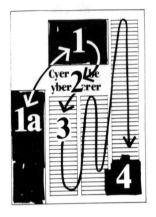

Lay Out for Function, Not Fad It is sad (and paradoxical with all the advertising talk about wanting to "be different") to notice how advertising layout—like so many other parts of advertising—moves in follow-the-crowd fads. Now and then, a fad just coincidentally turns out to the good. Not long ago, it seemed every advertisement had to have a headline set in Souvenir. Although the quirkiness of the "g" and "y" descenders and its generally "fat" appearance made the overuse noticeable (though not to many readers, I'm sure), Souvenir—because it is a near-traditional serif face and because advertisers normally set it in upper and lower case roman—is easily readable. So that fad did no harm.

But, starting in 1992, a deplorable body-copy-setting disease seemed to be spreading. *Particularly* deplorable in terms of one of the concerns of this chapter: using layout to make copy easy to flow through. The then emerging bad fad set the copy in low point size—often in a face with long ascenders and descenders, making small letter-bodies and adding to reading difficulty. It generally ran the copy "wall-to-wall," full length across a page (I have measured 30 and more picas, far too long for such small type sizes). And— affectation to end all affectations—the new fad leaded the lines so heavy (*some 50 to 90 points!*) that each line seemed to have nothing to do with the others! Leafing through just one issue of a magazine at the time when the fad was just starting, I found seven such lemmings. Then, to illustrate this new silliness, I set this example myself:

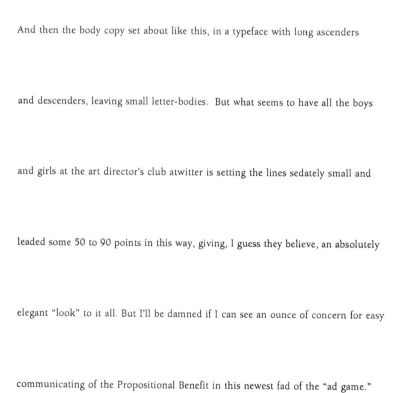

THE NEWEST LAYOUT FAD
FEATURES ALL CAPS IN AN
UNDERSIZED HEADLINE
WITH ALL LINES CENTERED,
SET REGULAR OR LIGHT

And then the body copy set about like this, in a typeface with long ascenders

and descenders, leaving small letter-bodies. But what seems to have all the boys

and girls at the art director's club atwitter is setting the lines sedately small and

leaded some 50 to 90 points in this way, giving, I guess they believe, an absolutely

elegant "look" to it all. But I'll be damned if I can see an ounce of concern for easy

communicating of the Propositional Benefit in this newest fad of the "ad game."

And, beyond belief until you see it, advertisers sometimes ran a headline *between the lines*. This called for a declaration of incompetence, if not complete insanity. Without question, this silly artificiality worked (and works) against communicating a Propositional Benefit quickly, easily, and clearly.

Believe it

Also, believe it or not, the copy, set in a low point size and in an italic regular

or not,

and leaded at least seventy-two points, ran all the way through the page like

the headline of

this, leaving the reader to figure out which he or she was supposed to read

the advertisement

first; but no matter which he or she decided to read first, this awful affectation

ran between the lines

of copy and headline setting style made it extremely difficult for him or her

of the copy all the way

to read either one easily. Obviously, this art director did not have easy, easy

through the page.

communications in mind, but, rather, creating "something really different."

Lines, Arrows, and Numbers I expect many art directors to consider it simplistic to use such things as lines, arrows, or numbers to help move eyes to where they should go (and to keep them from skidding someplace when they shouldn't). But I cannot imagine *readers* scoffing at these devices. Besides, if they work, what is lost?

Over the years, my good friends at Ralston Purina have invited me to make suggestions on their advertising. From personal experience and observation, I rank Ralston Purina as an exceptionally imaginative and at the same time pragmatic—thus highly successful—print advertiser. And no doubt this willingness, this confidence to learn from others—of course, not just from me—is one reason for its great print record. But I once found one of Purina's advertisements difficult to track as its creators intended. Although it contained, in essence, two columns, I felt people would not easily see it that way:

With permission of Ralston Purina Co.

I thought readers would read straight across the headline as "BEEF. BULL." They would not, as intended, read "BEEF," then read down to the Purina PRIME™ box, and then go back up to read "BULL," seeing it as a heading debunking all the claims below *that* word.

With permission of Ralston Purina Co.

I felt that simply running a line down between the "columns," the way some newspapers run rules between their columns, made you read that Purina PRIME™ is "BEEF" and that all the other claims about the *taste* of beef are "BULL," which is the proposition of the advertisement. Being the down-to-earth people they are, they amicably agreed.

From many experiences, I can tell you that, whenever appropriate, putting large numbers on sequential parts of your advertisement will give you two advantages: (1) In terms of this chapter's aim, people's eyes will naturally and easily follow the sequence you want them to follow for quick, easy, and full reading of the proposition. (2) As you will read in Chapter 7, large numbers in an advertisement work as a Laid-On Benefit that attracts interest.

Shape of Unit Affects Flow When we lay out an advertisement for, say, a magazine page, we usually start by drawing four lines that form a *vertical* rectangle. (This is logical, since magazines are rectangular.) Then we lay out the advertisement *within* those lines. If we think first of the interior elements we want to include (headlines, illustrations, copy, logo), and think of how we want people to track through these elements, we might find that a different exterior shape works better. That would be following the architectural principle of "form follows function"—the exterior shape of the building created by the best arrangement of the interior units. In advertising, following the principle of *format* following function, the exterior shape of an advertisement unit can come from the best arrangement of the interior elements.

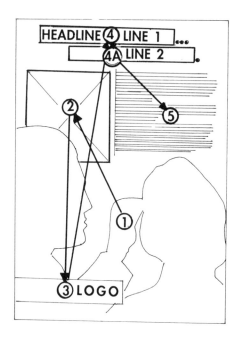

For example, here is a sketch of the layout for an advertisement as it ran in a *vertical* rectangular shape like the magazine page it filled. During a seminar session with the advertiser, we critiqued it, noting that it was a "two-step" or two-part advertisement. (The first line of the headline related to one picture—step one—and the second headline line related to the other picture—step two). Because of that, we concluded that designing it into a vertical rectangular shape did not produce a layout that easily tracked from element to element as desired. Instead, eyes probably started and moved as the numbers indicate, glancing first at two visually strong illustrations and a bold logo "panel" (1, 2, and 3), reading the two-part headline (4 and 4A) as a single unit without relating each part to the illustration to which it was supposed to refer, and then reading the copy (5). That, we all agreed, was not the sequence they wanted, nor one that quickly, easily, and fully unfolded the proposition.

Together, we decided that we wanted the elements to be seen and read in the following sequence: First, the major art with the first line of the headline, then the secondary art with the second line of the headline, then the copy, and finally the logo. When we arranged the elements that way, the result was a *horizontal* rectangle, which, in the magazine, would have been two lower half-pages side-by-side. This produced a layout not only impossible *not* to flow through as desired, but also one that added clarity and emphasis to the two steps of the message.

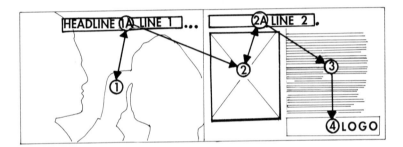

KISS

However you do it—in the usual vertical or in a horizontal shape; with or without the aid of lines, arrows, or numbers; with headline over, under, or alongside the picture; etc.— always remember that THE primary purposes of layout are to (1) get some benefit for pausing instantly seen and then (2) make it EASY for readers' eyes to flow through the advertisement to get the Propositional Benefit quickly and completely. Along with using the few tips in this chapter, you serve those purposes best when you "*Keep It Simple, Sam or Samantha.*"

The Laid-On Benefit: When the Propositional Benefit Needs Help

7

As we have noted, every advertisement makes a proposition: "Do this to enjoy this benefit." I call that the Propositional Benefit—the benefit derived from doing what the advertisement proposes. To get people to pause and stop, we can (and should) feature the Propositional Benefit (1) when we introduce a new or improved product and (2) until we feel sure "everybody knows" the product's proposition.

But for a mature product's year-in, year-out brand equity advertising, there comes a time when the product's proposition no longer rates as noteworthy news, or no longer enjoys any form of exclusivity, or no longer is a big deal (if it ever was). After years of use, it remains a perfectly legitimate but not, in itself, a high-impact proposition. It becomes simply a "use-this-product-for-the-good-reason-you-know-so-well" proposal. Or, at any time in the product life, the Propositional Benefit may be a bit too complex to give a single quick-and-easy-to-understand-as-a-benefit signal of it.

That's when the Laid-On Benefit comes in. At its best, the Laid-On Benefit can redeliver the familiar Propositional

Benefit in a new and especially memorable way. At minimum, it can get a pause and stop long enough for another noting-in-passing of a proposition already well known.

The Laid-On Benefit works through the *execution* of the advertisement, an execution that, *in itself*, offers some momentary benefit such as:

- Enjoyment of some form of "entertainment"
- Quick and easy satisfaction of aroused curiosity
- Admiration of beauty
- Intrigue of an ingenious word or word/picture play
- Appeal of a fresh verbalization or visualization

Thus, the Propositional Benefit is the benefit promised by *the product*. A Laid-On Benefit is a momentary benefit provided immediately *by the advertisement*. But, and note this, while you can *start* and *finish* with a Propositional Benefit, you can only *start* with a Laid-On Benefit. You must—I repeat, *must*—go on to deliver the Propositional Benefit—else, why run the advertisement?

Now, let's separate the "pause" from the "stop" to note another important point about the Laid-On Benefit. To get a "pause," a Laid-On Benefit *need not have anything to do with the Propositional Benefit* (as long as it is not incompatible with the proposition, and, as a result, either moves people off zero in the wrong direction or conflicts with the intended "tone" of the proposition).

I never go alone.
But I always go Stag.

With permission of White Stag Manufacturing Co.

An often-used such Laid-On Benefit is to make the page appear to have been torn, as White Stag did with this advertisement—which also used a second Laid-On Benefit of the same genre, the hand-written headline. Both the seemingly torn page and the handwriting aroused curiosity ("Why is the page torn?" "What did somebody write on the page?"), and the advertisement offers, as the benefit for pausing, quick and easy satisfaction of this curiosity ("I can find out with a glance.").

Given today's production technology, we can use many variations on the torn page: Make the page appear to have been partly burned, make it look wet, wrinkled, or transparent—if you can think of it, they can do it. Such ploys, however, will get only split-second pauses, which may be long enough for what I called another "noting-in-passing" of the familiar proposition, but not much more. Which leads to a second important point about Laid-On Benefits, and the second purpose for them.

With permission of EL AL Israel Airlines, Ltd.

The Laid-On Benefit that gets a "stop" almost always relates to the Propositional Benefit, as it did when EL AL used the torn-page format not only to get people to pause, but also to get them to stop for this dramatic and memorable presentation of the proposition to fly EL AL because it had bought new airplanes that crossed the Atlantic Ocean 20% faster. Their advertisement is now a classic: **On December 23 the Atlantic Ocean became 20% smaller.** And it's a classic solution to the problem presented when the Propositional Benefit is a bit too complex (what kind of airplanes EL AL bought) for a quick-and-easy-to-understand-as-a-benefit signal of it.

Before we examine several more forms of Laid-On Benefits, note these additional essential-to-know points about them:

1. Although using a Laid-On Benefit often results in an advertisement that is "clever" in some way, it must still follow the rule that clarity comes *before* cleverness. For the simple and irrefutable reason that if they don't understand it, they *cannot* find it clever. (Why don't outsiders laugh at inside jokes?)

2. A Laid-On Benefit must *not* do two things, and *must* do two others:

   • **Must-Not:** Overpower the Propositional Benefit to the point where people remember the Laid-On Benefit device or method, but not the Propositional Benefit. (Everyone remembered a pop-up advertisement that formed the skyline of downtown San Francisco. But my own survey of 100 people did not find one who remembered who ran the advertisement or what it was selling.)

   • **Must-Not:** Be a silly, senseless gimmick that does nothing to communicate the proposition or, worse, actually works against it. (An advertisement by a boot maker showed a woman with two normal legs and a third leg growing out of her pelvic area, with each leg wearing a boot. The effect was grotesque. She did not look, as intended, like a "with-it" woman wearing terrific boots. She looked like a circus geek!)

   • **Must:** Get people to pause—otherwise, why use it?

   • **Must:** Allow a fast and smooth segue from the Laid-On Benefit to the Propositional Benefit.

Creative Opportunities in Print

I am always delighted and re-enthused about the creative opportunities of my medium when I see still another innovative form of Laid-On Benefit. In the space permitted by this book, I can share with you only a small portion of my files. But I want you to see and read about enough of them to fix in your mind what they are—and also, hope-fully, to delight and enthuse (or re-enthuse) you with the opportunities for imaginative work in print.

The Ever-Appealing Quiz People can't resist quizzes anywhere, especially quizzes they find in the privacy of reading. One of the top-rated features in *Reader's Digest*—from the month it started—is the quiz, **Enrich Your Word Power**. Five times, over a period of some 15 years, the *Digest* ran articles titled **Are You A Genius?** with quizzes to take. Each time, Mensa, the international organization for people with genius-range IQ's, received sacks of mail—tens of thousands of completed quizzes sent in with the question, "Do I qualify?" If tens of thousands scored high enough to do that, imagine how many *millions* took the quizzes—on five separate occasions!

So, if you can logically put your advertisement in the form of a little quiz, it makes a great Laid-On Benefit. "Lit-tle" because, of course, in advertising it should not be long or serious. And it cannot be a humorless and transparent set-up designed to force people into giving "good answers" about your product. You *can* get them to do that—in fact, you always *try* to—but with good humor, perhaps whimsy, as Kool-Aid did so waggishly with this advertisement using the Laid-On Benefit of a fun little quiz.

HINT: It's the one with Vitamin C and no caffein...
HINT: It's the one with fruity flavors kids love...
HINT: It's the one that's only ½ the price of soda¹...
HINT: It's the one for kids...

With permission of General Foods U.S.A.

Almost as appealing as a quiz is anything that people have a bit of fun "figuring out" (and then feel elated with themselves because they "got it"—like getting a word in a crossword puzzle). It was love at first sight when I spotted the headline written for a dealer advertisement by Volkswagen of America. No way could you *not* stop to "figure it out"—and what a great job it did in dramatizing its Propositional Benefit, as shown at left.

We'll stop y ur VW engine fr m miss ng.

Follow the Numbers In Chapter 6, I suggested the use of large numbers as a way to get eyes to track through a layout as you want them to. Such numbers work well as a Laid-On Benefit because (1) numbers on a page help create an "active look," (2) they help create an impression that the advertisement will give you specific information, and (3) they arouse curiosity ("What's numbered, and why?").

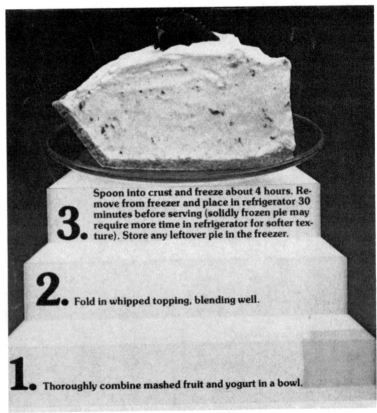

3. Spoon into crust and freeze about 4 hours. Remove from freezer and place in refrigerator 30 minutes before serving (solidly frozen pie may require more time in refrigerator for softer texture). Store any leftover pie in the freezer.

2. Fold in whipped topping, blending well.

1. Thoroughly combine mashed fruit and yogurt in a bowl.

With permission of General Foods U.S.A.

The instant your eyes see this Cool Whip advertisement, your eyes go to the numbers, and—you can't keep your eyes from doing it—they move up the 1, 2, and 3 to the pie. True, when they get there, they may not stay. You might or might not be interested in the instructions for how to make the pie. But remember that if a Laid-On Benefit gets even a pause, it has done its job. And, as your eyes sweep up those numbers, you have certainly paused, if not stopped.

Graphic Presentation You turn a page and see what appears to be a hand-lettered headline that someone has tried to erase. (No, it does not break the rule that advertising headlines must be easy to read. They made sure it was still easy to read even with the "erasing," which, of course, makes you curious to read it.) And, in addition to making you pause and stop, doesn't it do a grand job of helping to make quickly, easily—and memorably—clear the Propositional Benefit of Maxell recording tape? (From the headline alone, you know what that proposed benefit will be—and the copy quickly explains how Maxell tape delivers the Propositional Benefit promised.)

With permission of Maxell Corp. of America

Ask Them to Do Something You scan-read this headline with two visual gulps: You look around. Nobody's watching. So you put your hand over the picture. (Why? Human nature, bless it.) In putting your hand over the picture, you have stopped (as the Laid-On Benefit of curiosity quickly and easily satisfied was designed to get you to do). And, in the process, you gave yourself an impressive demonstration of "how small the world's smallest standard cassette recorder is"—a demonstration of the Propositional Benefit (something else Laid-On benefits can do).

With permission of Sony Corp. of America

Scratch 'n' Sniff Nothing A bona fide scratch 'n' sniff advertisement is a very expensive Laid-On Benefit (satisfaction of curiosity) and demonstration of the Propositional Benefit (with the scent encapsulated into the ink). But a recent consumer movement away from scented products (Unscented Tide, unscented Dove, etc.) opened the door for a number of opportunistic advertisers who printed the typical scratch 'n' sniff panels on their advertisements, but without the scent encapsulation. When readers scratched and sniffed (paused and stopped), they, of course, smelled nothing—exactly the Propositional Benefit offered. Ergo, a Laid-On Benefit once again does double duty: (1) makes readers pause/stop and (2) quickly, easily, and memorably delivers the Propositional Benefit.

Common Characteristics
of Good Laid-On Benefits

Even from just the few examples I have shown and described, I hope you noted that Laid-On Benefits can take
many different forms. But note also these fundamental *sim-
ilarities* among most good Laid-On Benefits:

- The layouts of most Laid-On Benefits are such that
  they immediately either (1) arouse curiosity or (2)
  promise a bit of verbal or visual "entertainment."
- The layouts also clearly signal that it will be quick and
  easy for you to satisfy your curiosity or enjoy the bit
  of "entertainment."
- Your curiosity is properly satisfied. You feel "that was
  worth pausing/stopping for," and never "Why did I
  stop for that stupid trick?" Or, if you *are* tricked, it is
  done in a way that makes you chuckle—never in a way
  that makes you feel "taken."
- If it is the promise of a bit of "entertainment" that
  makes you pause/stop, you do, indeed, enjoy the bit of
  "entertainment."
- The best Laid-On Benefits, in addition to making you
  pause/stop, also actually deliver the Propositional Benefit quickly, easily—and *memorably*.
- Or, if they don't deliver it, they (1) are compatible with
  the nature of the Propositional Benefit, and (2) permit
  a quick and "natural" segue from the Laid-On to the
  Propositional Benefit.

Underlying Generalization In Chapter 11, I will write
that a common quality of all great print advertisements
is "heart." They all exude good will and friendliness;
they clearly like, thus respect, people. (Only public service advocacy advertisements can scold and/or be stern—
e.g., "It's stupid to use drugs.") It seems to me—and not
surprisingly—that the same good will/friendliness rule applies to Laid-On Benefits. If you create them in that spirit,
all the above falls into place.

In this Jim Beam advertisement, for example, you easily satisfied your curiosity and *enjoyed* tracing through the popularity of hamburgers in 1955, BLTs in 1959, Dagwoods in 1968, grinders in 1975, pitas in 1983, croissants in 1987 and back to hamburgers in 1990—coming back, as Jim Beam proposed, "to the basics." Although this advertisement lured you into another registration of the Jim Beam proposition, its friendly tone kept you from feeling the least bit "taken."

With permission of James B. Beam Distilling Co. via Fallon McElligott

Conclusion Re Cleverness

The bulk of advertising is for products with universally or near-universally known propositions. Hence many advertisements use Laid-On Benefits. Laid-On Benefits often demand some form of cleverness. Hence many advertisements that you see exhibit such cleverness. That can lead to a wrong conclusion and to one of those cliché notions that we must forget (i.e., that advertisement must always be "clever"). In thoroughly professional advertisements, you do not—I repeat, do *not*—find the cleverness there just because, "Hey, man, that's what advertising is all about." You find it there only when needed, and needed for an absolutely *pragmatic* reason: to get a pause, a stop, and a reading necessary to obtain another registration—and/or a fresh registration—of a widely and well-known proposition. Thus, Laid-On Benefits (hence also cleverness) are by no means ends in themselves. They serve, when needed, to help achieve the primary objective of all advertising: To make the Propositional Benefit quickly, easily, and fully clear.

How
to Write
Headlines

8

"**H**ow to Keep Young Mentally"
"Love—Luxury or Necessity?"
"What Kind of Husband Are You?"
"Useful Points in Judging People"
"Can We Have a Beautiful Human Race?"
"Advice From a President's Physician"

Excellent headlines all. And all—plus two dozen more equally good—from the very first *Reader's Digest* table of contents. All written back in 1922.

And they have been as good—so often *great*—during all the years since. So when I got the assignment to analyze how *Digest* editors used print so successfully, what a resource I had from which to draw to study headlines (which they call "titles"). A resource to which I later added hundreds of *advertising* headlines, learning in the process what I have used, successfully I believe, for nearly 40 years—and offer you in this chapter: how to write headlines that (1) get read and understood fast and (2) interest the greatest number of people with the greatest intensity of interest.

What It Takes

A good writer is not only someone who can string words together skillfully—not even if you add "beautifully" to "skillfully." A good writer also, and maybe *more* so, is someone who can come up with just the right thing to say. In fact, if we change "*good* writer" to "*interesting* writer," then content surely ranks higher than does word selection and arrangement.

91

And that applies even more than normally to writing headlines. Because with a headline you have no opportunity to add another sentence to strengthen the meaning or impact of the one before. No opportunity to add an "e.g." or an "i.e." or anything in parentheses. You write it, put it "out there," and that's it. Thus, headline writing demands a great deal of "*before*-writing" thought. I divide the discipline into two steps:

Step 1: *What* you will say—with all the thinking that goes into this decision.

Step 2: *How* you will say it—with all the fundamentals, techniques, skills, and artistry that go into the writing part of it.

As with most all steps of any mental process, I of course do *not* mean separate sequential steps. Yes, you think before you write, but certainly you think *while* you write, and you may do some trial writing to help you think. So the process is more a matter of steps taken simultaneously or near simultaneously, with a good deal of back-and-forth.

What You Will Say

When I work on a headline, I imagine myself at a party, sitting next to a stranger with whom I want to open a conversation on a subject (the subject for which I am seeking a headline). As I think of and/or write different trial headlines, I try to visualize what sort of response I might get from that person. For example, if I sense I would get a blank look, I know I am not being clear enough. If I would be embarrassed to say it, I know it is in bad taste or too intimate, and so on. *Anyone,* unless he or she is an insensitive clod, can feel first-hand the reaction to what they *say* in conversation. But so many people seem to lose that sensitivity when writing.

Start from Where They Are Yes, obviously, this is the same rule as for the advertisement as a whole, and logically so because the headline helps start the advertisement. Suppose I asked that imaginary person-at-a-party, "Have you heard the latest on over-drinking?" In my exercise, I can imagine the person gripping his or her drink, glaring at me and gritting, "Do I look like an over-drinker?" But imagine me holding up my *own* drink and saying, "I read something interesting about when *this* sort of drinking moves over the line to *over*-drinking." Now I can see the person glancing at his or her *own* drink, smiling and asking, "Oh? When is that?"

There you have all the "before-writing" editorial thinking about "where they are" that made *Reader's Digest* change the headline of an article condensed out of another magazine from **LATEST ON OVER-DRINKING** to **When Does Social Drinking Become Over-Drinking?**

Do you remember, too, from Chapter 3, "where they are *at this time?*" During some seminars, I show a slide of a young woman wearing a bridal veil, with the headline, **Would you risk washing your hair on your wedding day?** When I first started to show it years ago, I could feel (actually *see*) the women in the audience drawing in their breath as if to say, "My God, NO!" But (and I keep using the slide precisely to note the change), these days, I hear them chuckling at the "quaintness" of the advertisement. With the new shampoos and conditioners and especially hair dryers, yes, of course, they *would indeed* wash their hair on their wedding day.

Silly Question Department In advertising headlines, one of the most often seen forms of *not* starting from where people are reminds me of those *New Yorker* filler-features, "Questions we doubt ever got asked." Only these headlines are questions advertisers *want* answered, but about which readers could not care less. **WHO JUDGED TEGRIN'S MEDICATED INGREDIENT EFFECTIVE?** no doubt got, and deserved, the mental response (*if* anyone stopped to read it), "Who cares?" The same response for **Why is any size headache The Excedrin Headache?** If you were known to be associated with those products, can you even imagine yourself sitting down next to someone at a party and asking such self-centered questions?

Where They Are in *Every* Way Also from Chapter 3, do you recall my emphasis upon knowing or sensing where people are in *every* way—some of the "ways" being subtleties? For some examples:

- What is *immediately meaningful* to them? If people see, for a compact car, a well-known football player saying in the headline: **NOW I CAN GAIN 466,400 YARDS ON JUST ONE TANKFUL**, will they immediately view that number of yards as a lot of miles? (Quick, how many yards in a mile?)

- As they view things, are they *likely to agree with you?* An advertisement showed a woman holding a bowl of big, red-ripe strawberries over a headline **IT'S GOOD, BUT IT'S NOT DESSERT.** The point was supposed to be that she didn't consider it dessert without a topping of an artificial whipped cream. But when it's common for a waiter to say, "We have some beautiful fresh strawberries," and for weight-conscious diners to reply, "Great! I'll have just the berries," to call a bowl full of them "not dessert" certainly misses where an awful lot of people are.

- What will they *likely believe?* About a television set (among the so many available today) will people believe that it is **THE NEW PICTURE EVERYONE'S RUSHING TO SEE?** I seriously doubt it. Or, about a cigarette, the headline **Demand Builds for Merit Taste Technology?** Would they believe that (assuming they understood it)?

- What will they view as *something they want?* Are people so concerned with the amount of electricity used by the clocks in their house that they will look eagerly for **Atmos... The only clock in the world powered by air?** Do you think many people so regret that they plan to buy a moped that they will jump at the chance to learn **How to convince yourself to buy a Kawasaki KE100 instead of a moped?**

- What might inadvertently put your creative foot in your mouth? When I saw this headline, **SOME OF E.F. HUTTON'S SMARTEST CUSTOMERS ARE WOMEN,** my immediate thought was would they have written a headline saying some of their smartest customers were *men?* I don't think so, but I'm sure many women were not at all complimented by the implication that some of them being smart made news so unusual as to be worthy of an advertising headline.

Say Something! When trying to write a headline, another discipline I apply is to start by ignoring (for the moment) such things as wording, active verbs, rhythm—all the skills and techniques that go into writing—and simply write down what I call a *"generic headline."* This comes out of asking myself, "What do I want to say, to communicate?" (And I don't consider it giving up when I find, as I so often do, that I cannot improve on that generic headline.)

To help make more people more familiar with and less intimidated by personal computers, I wrote a plain-language,

12-page advertisement for IBM that (testing later showed) did a good job of taking the mystery out of such frightening terms and concepts as binary code, programming, and "a machine with memory" (Big Brother!). For my generic headline, I wrote, **Only what it will help you to know about how a computer works.**

With that in front of me, I could not possibly write a meaningless label headline such as **Computer Common Sense.** Nor could I strain to write some equally meaningless thing that I thought clever, such as **PC on PC: Personal Counsel on Personal Computers.** When the booklet-type advertisement went into 50 million *Digest* homes, it carried the title at right.

The same emphasis on "saying something" made *Digest* editors change the headlines at left to those at right:

Only what it *helps* to know about how a computer works.

NOTHING REALLY HAPPENED	**If Your Child Is Molested**
TALKING DOWN	**Let's Stop Short-Changing Young Readers**
Step right up and test your wits on the thrills and spills of **SPELLING...** then try for the gold ring: **MEMORY**	**The 100 Words Easiest to Misspell**

And, in advertisements, the same emphasis makes me so greatly admire such content-full, thus meaningful, headlines as **Kids stay free at Travel Lodge.** And **We teach you how to be beautiful . . . free.**

When I see a headline as empty of meaning as **Chevron says YES** and then see what it says in the subhead, I want to use the subhead as the headline and have it say this:

The Balancing Act How do you interest the greatest *number* of people with the greatest *intensity* of interest? It's a balancing act because what you do for the greatest *number* works against what you do for the greatest *intensity* and vice versa.

When we service your car we give 6 guarantees.

Do you get all 6 now?

- To interest the greatest number of people, you try to make your headline as general as possible.
- To get the greatest intensity of interest, you try to make your headline as specific as possible.

So you end up asking yourself, "How specific can I get and still interest a mass audience?"

In another publication **Why Some Men Live Longer** makes a headline with strong interest to all men and, in varying degrees and for different reasons, to some women. But the article centered entirely on *one* killer of *both* men and women, the heart. The *Digest* titled it **The Secret of a Stronger Heart**. Now that aims from the start and directly at *both* men and women (as opposed to at men primarily and only secondarily at women). And it has much more intense interest to all people concerned with heart problems or actually suffering them—a mass audience.

Suppose you saw a headline reading **Cross-Country Skiing: The Best Exercise**. If, as I do, you viewed that as having intense interest —or any interest at all—to only a relatively small number of people, how would you change it to get a much larger audience, but still with strong interest? Well, which are the interest-limiting words? Do you agree they are "Cross-Country Skiing?" Your advertisement is intended to enlarge the market for a product (skis or an exercise machine). But think of all those people with whom it might succeed. What do most of them start out wanting more, to cross-country ski or to get the best exercise? The best exercise, right? So **The Single Best Exercise You Can Do** would certainly have intense interest, and to a greater number than the original headline. (Nordic Track is, at this writing, making a fortune with just that approach. I use one, but surely not because I want to cross-country ski vicariously—I dread those 20-minute sessions—but I want that best exercise.)

The Ralston Purina people, whom I have already cited in this book and a number of times through the years as astute print advertisers, once again demonstrated their astuteness when they ran an eight-page booklet-type advertisement, which they could have headlined **A Pet Owner's Guide**. Instead, they laid out the multipage advertisement so that, after you detached it for reading and reference, you could read four of the pages starting with a cover showing cats with the headline **A Cat Owner's Guide**, then turn it around and read the other four pages starting with a cover showing dogs with the headline **A Dog Owner's Guide**. Thus they got two mass audiences (plus a third audience owning both dogs and cats), and got them all with the greatest possible intensity of interest—a brilliant accomplishment!

How **You Say It**

Write First for Clarity "For sake of greater clarity" ranks as one of the most common reasons why *Reader's Digest* changes titles of articles. Note the titles from other publications at left and the *Digest*'s at right for the same articles:

Clues to a Deadly Riddle   Is Cancer Infectious?

Chronic Fatigue Syndrome   ARE YOU TIRED OR SICK?

An advertisement for a camera that shot both normal focus and close-ups without complicated resettings showed two such photographs under a headline **Double Take**. This was obviously an attempted play on *taking* pictures, but, to me, it was a risky one since, in photography, "double" has a negative connotation (double exposure). And, because doing a "double take" means glancing at something, turning away, and then instantly turning back—which, of course, has nothing to do with the proposition—I considered that headline as meaningless and even confusing. It would have been better, certainly more clear, to simply headline each picture as **Normal/Close-Up**. My friends at Kodak, who had asked for the comment, agreed.

Suppose you were shown layout and copy for an advertisement, with the illustration including a snapshot of a couple and a part of the snapshot (the heads of the couple) mounted on the face of a wristwatch. Suppose the headline said **If You've Got The Picture We've Got The Time**. Because the illustration of the snapshot and of the watch partly communicates the proposition, you might get away with that headline. But why chance it simply to indulge someone wanting to play with an old expression? People will either *want* a wristwatch with a family photo on the face or they *will not*. For those who will, the quicker they understand the proposition, the better. The essence, if not the wording, of a much clearer headline was in the first line of the copy: "**Just give us your favorite photo and we'll turn it into your favorite watch.**" I sigh when I see such things, knowing that, more often than not, such a suggestion will get a wail of, "You can't just say it as simple as tha-at!" Why not? In fact, as I repeat and repeat, when you're handed an interesting and appealing proposition, why do anything else?

Get *to* It Try to write headlines that put the most interesting words at the beginning. Always visualize those idly glancing page-turners with their minds "somewhere else," certainly not looking eagerly for your message. If they look at advertising headlines at all, they, as we all do, start with the first words. Perhaps those of us who write headlines would be better off if we had inferiority complexes about anyone paying attention to us—unless we *quickly* give them good reason to.

Such a phobia would have helped the writer who started a headline with **A GARLAND OF ENVIES**...because the rest of it was the interesting words...**or 21 reasons why I wish I were a MAN**. Interesting if idly glancing eyes ever got to them. That's why the *Digest* got right to the point with its title *I Wish I Were a Man*! (Intensely interesting enough for any woman without the specificity of the "21 reasons"—some of which the *Digest* left out anyway.)

"Getting to it" does not simplistically mean always just blurting out your main point. There are times when preliminary words are sufficiently interesting in themselves to hold readers while they (the preliminary words) give extra meaning and impact to the key word or words deliberately put at the end, as with the headline at left.

Kodak introduces a feature never before available on a high-speed walk-up copier.

Simplicity.

That worked because of the smart separation from the other lines of the word *Simplicity*. Also, the headline sat directly over a picture of the copiers. Since eyes almost always go to illustrations first, people probably read "Simplicity" as they looked at the picture. Thus Kodak and agency had their cake and ate it, too. They gave the word *Simplicity* the build-up that added significance to it, and they also got it read first...and then again last.

What I strongly discourage doing most often manifests itself in:

- Expecting readers to wade through a number of uninteresting (to readers) preliminary words before they get to the guts of the headline—the key words that *will* interest them.
- Putting first what the advertiser considers important—for example, the full product name and/or product description or slogan—rather than what readers will. This practice produces benefit-delayed headlines such as **New From Bug-Bug**™ **"The Spray That Makes Bugs Bug Off**©: *A SPRAY THAT'S OZONE SAFE!* (Name and claim entirely fictitious, and any similarity between them and any existing or contemplated names

and/or claims are coincidental, though I kind of like Bug-Bug and the slogan.)

Verb It "Label" headlines carry no verbs or no "verb feeling" even with a verb. To me, they come off as nothing more than the "names" of the subjects of articles or advertisements. As such, they arouse no more interest than do the product names on packages. Also, they look static and sterile, as opposed to active and fertile. Finally, they do not follow the good headline rule to "SAY something." For these reasons, *Reader's Digest* rewrote a title from **Solving Problems** to **Teach Your Mind to Think** and changed **World Population Growth** to **Population Growth Is Good**.

Similarly, in a corporate advertisement, I once saw an illustration of a giant new ship, a tanker, and the headline **Ship of Dreams**. After I read the copy and learned what it meant, I rewrote the headline to say **We've Placed a Huge Bet on America Coming Back!** Not only "verbing it," but active verbing it, which always beats any form of the verb "to be." If you admire David Ogilvy as I do, you might remember, as I do, that he could have written **At 60 miles an hour the loudest noise in this new Rolls Royce is from the electric clock.** But he wrote . . . *comes* **from the electric clock.**

Familiar Advice, Familiar Words After all I have already written about this principle in Chapter 4, I don't intend to spend much time or many words on it here. I will simply remind you that when people see familiar combinations of words in familiar sequence, they automatically apply a technique of speed-reading—they read in "visual gulps," not one word at a time but four, five, or even six. Visual gulps allow people to read and understand headlines quickly and easily, which I hope you always remember as an absolute necessity for advertising headlines.

Get "YOU" in Whenever it works naturally into familiar combinations of words, it helps to write in a "you." **What Happens When The Dollar Devalues** does not immediately give readers (average readers, not economists) a sense of personal involvement. But they get such a feeling from **Why Imported Products Now Cost You More**.

You won't always find it possible, or even desirable, to use the word "you" if it leads to a "contorted" headline. You cannot always—and don't always need to—use the actual word "you," but you should always *think* "you" (i.e., them, all those people out there) in your approach.

With a photograph of men moving airliner seats (you don't know if the men are removing or installing the seats) ran the headline **TWA unseats the competition.** That supposed piece of cleverness has no "you" in it, either in wording or approach. (It's a "who cares" headline, to boot). But a subhead line in the advertisement had a "you" approach, and should have been the headline: **Wider seats and more legroom than any other airline.**

Sure, Go for the Heart and the Funny Bone Now and then, when it seems right, pull out the stops, get emotional, wear your heart on your sleeve. Yes, you risk going too far, overdoing it, and ending up on the corny side. (Young readers: Don't worry about that. Sophistication *does* come with age and experience, and someday you will "just know" how far to go. But don't *start* sterile—you may stay that way!)

DeWitt Wallace instilled this kind of sophistication into *Digest* editing from the start. He loved sentiment and hated sentimentality. Thus, *Digest* editors "just knew" how far to go in changing the label **One Mother's Legacy** to the more dramatic **The Day I Met My Mother.** And in changing the not-bad **Vigil For a Little Boy** to the more powerful **Please God, Don't Take Travis**!

Similarly, I enthusiastically applaud advertisement headlines that enhance what they say by how they say it. Two provisos: (1) when doing so is appropriate or (2) when a straight statement of the proposition will no longer get a pause and a stop, and the more colorful wording of the headline provides a Laid-On Benefit. For a few examples, headlines that are, to good effect:

Humorous:

We could tell you all the ways Federal Agents use SkyPagers. But then we'd have to kill you.

Possession of a lawyer is nine-tenths of the law.

Whimsical:

A marshmallow a day makes your blue eyes bluer.

BEING OVERWEIGHT IS NOT HEREDITARY. BUT IT DOES SHOW UP IN THE JEANS.

Playful:

GO OUT AND HUG A ROAD YOU LIKE
(for a sporty car)

Why pay cash for batteries when you can charge it?
(for rechargeable batteries)

Surprising:

Turn this magazine 12 times.
There, you just made home-made ice cream.
(for a new, easy ice cream maker)

Chivas Regal is always twelve years old.
                    Rarely thirteen.

Trenchant:

God didn't give His only begotten Son to be a spokesman for the Moral Majority.
(For the Episcopal Church with a photograph of Jesus in a pin-striped suit.)

Most young car thieves start your car the same way you do.
(With your keys.)

Will a Graphic Help? Take an excellent speech, and you can make it better with a delivery using expressive hands and face, and most often even better with visual aids. When you write headlines, always ask yourself if some sort of graphic will make it even better.

If you read only the words of the headline **How To Be Your Dog's Best Friend,** you might, from the twist on what is whose best friend, get some impression that it titled a humorous article. But isn't that impression strengthened by running the headline around this piece of art?

Note what only a *touch* of graphics can do—how the Bible-like illumination of the "Q" so greatly enhances the meaning of the headline:

How To Be Your Dog's Best Friend

Questions People Ask Ministers Most

Pepto-Bismol®, announcing that "you get a handy easy-measure dose cup" with its new plastic bottle, could have, to a public thoroughly accustomed to taking the medication with a spoon, communicated its proposition with only the headline **No Spoon Necessary**. But doesn't that headline get wonderful help with the international symbol for "no-something"? (They made it even more meaningful by printing the symbol in Pepto-Bismol pink.)

With permission of 3M

For this great 3M Filtrete™ filter advertisement, either the art director also wrote the headline, or the copywriter also did the art, or those two people have a wonderfully synergistic way of working together. This headline says as much with the graphics as it does with words. The dog, the cat, the dust (the terrific touch of "finger-lettering" two of the headline words in it), the pipe smoke, the ragweed—words and graphics together say it far more vividly than either could have alone. I view 3M as a superb company in so many ways, including print advertising.

Will a Subhead Help? Magazine editors greatly help their titles with what they call "blurbs" and advertising people call subheads. If the magazine title or the advertisement headline are the "pause/stop getters," the blurb or subhead can give significant help as the "quick orienter" that adds meaning to the title/headline and pulls people into the text/copy. In addition, blurbs and subheads make easier the eye transition from the large headline type to the much smaller copy type size. Though I have looked, I have not found a truly good use of a subhead in an advertisement— I think advertising misses a good bet in not using them more.

Note how the blurb under this *Digest* title "fleshes out" the headline and moves you in an interest-intensifying step ("five common issues") from the headline into the article, completely oriented and ready to take it in:

What You Should Know Before You Remarry

The failure rate for remarriages is even higher than for the first ones. Here are five common issues that should be faced before you take that second step.

Do You Need a Headline at All? At least twice, maybe three times, written on men's room walls, I have seen, read—and each time lost—the bet as worded at right.

I'll bet you ten dollars that you will read all the way down to here

Also, I have seen (and greatly admired) advertisements with no headlines. They have lured me into starting the copy, and then I could not (actually *did not want to*) stop. Obviously, this demands excellent writing, both in style and content. In addition, it requires a specific writing style and layout/typography:

- The text must be set very large (for copy—around 18 to 24 points in magazines, maybe larger in full-size newspapers).
- You must lay out the copy so that eyes go first and naturally to the beginning and flow effortlessly through it.
- You must use an exceptionally easy-to-read typeface, set in an equally easy-to-read way.
- You must write short, easy-to-scan-read, and easy-to-understand sentences.
- The "story line" must flow smoothly, and in a straight, easy-to-follow sequence, with no detours.

Write for Rhythm I have written poetry all my life. And, during the years when I wrote advertisements every day, I kept a copy of Robert Frost on my bedside table, reading randomly most every night. Alternately, I did the same with an anthology of Shakespeare. In addition, I studied— I *worked* at studying—Winston Churchill's speeches. I wanted to retain and continue developing my feeling for rhythm in writing, so that when I wrote something— especially a headline—it would move along with the beat I intended, and when it was finished, you knew it. Just like that sentence.

Keep rhythm in mind, too, as you apply what you have learned from this chapter. If you do, perhaps someday, you will thrill yourself by writing a headline as rhythmic and inspired as this one promoting tourism in Scotland (run with a tartan-colorful, soul-swirling photograph of pipers piping and marching right at you):

When the lads are piping
with all their hearts
you feel you're marching
off to glory!

How
to Condense

9

Prophetically, DeWitt Wallace, who dropped out of two colleges, got his education (a *superb* one) out of magazines. And, in the process, first germinated and later developed and refined a new editing art form: *Reader's Digest condensing.* How he did it not only makes interesting reading but also gives you the right perspective on this skill, which *Digest* editors apply and which you can put to such good use in advertising.

Charlie Ferguson, long-time *Digest* editor, recorded that Wally devoured magazines and once wrote to his father (president of one of the colleges from which Wally dropped out): "I have 3×5 inch slips of paper, and when I read an article I place all the facts I wish to preserve or remember on one of these slips. Before going to sleep at night, I mentally review what I've read during the day." Wally added (probably defensively to his Ph.D, D.D., LL.D. father, who considered him a drifter), "I don't see why time thus spent is not as beneficial as if spent studying books."

Ferguson reported also: "Sometimes a quote or a simple outline didn't suffice. Wally would then copy down . . . the *essence* of the article as a whole, *condensing it in the writer's own words*" (my italics).

After dropping out of his second college, Wallace went to work for a St. Paul company that published agricultural textbooks. At night, he continued his reading and note taking. That's when he first started thinking about a magazine—one offering "*distilled* business counsel and pointers for achieving success" (my italics).

Birth of THE Idea Months of work on the idea produced a 128-page booklet, *Getting the Most Out of Farming*—the ancestor of *Reader's Digest.* Driving through five states, Wallace sold 100,000 copies to banks and seed stores to give to customers. Then, while considering follow-ups (e.g., one for storekeepers, condensing the best merchandising articles), Wally got THE idea: a magazine for *all* readers "digesting" informative, useful articles.

World War I put all this on hold for a while. But after Sgt. Wallace suffered near-fatal shrapnel wounds during the Meuse-Argonne offensive, he had months of ambulatory convalescence in an Army hospital filled with magazines! As Ferguson wrote, "He now concentrated on the idea: Reading, selecting articles, boiling them down as he copied them in his chisel-clear handwriting."

Six months after his discharge, Wallace had "a stockpile of choice articles" from which he selected 31—each cut to *two pages or less*—and had the first dummy copies of a reader's digest printed. He hoped to sell the idea to any publisher who would hire him as editor. But, one after the other, the big publishers of that time (including William Randolph Hearst) turned him down. So, in 1922, he took two momentous steps: He married Lila Acheson, who deeply loved Wallace and believed in his idea. And (to hell with the big publishers!), the two of them would launch *Reader's Digest* themselves!

During that first year, when the Wallaces lived and worked at No. 1 Minetta Lane in Greenwich Village, Wallace went every day to the New York Public Library to use the magazines available there. He searched for articles "of lasting interest," and, writing on yellow sheets of paper, he, as Ferguson described it, *"eliminated asides, pruned wordy prose, got straight to the point"* (my italics). And out of all this thinking, experimenting, and doing came a new editing art form. Far more sophisticated than mere abridgement, it flowed smoothly from beginning to end, with no obvious "amputations" of sections, faithfully retaining the style and the essential message of the original writer.

Today, over 100 million readers a month enjoy *Digest* condensing in 17 languages. (Yes, the basic techniques of condensing work in *all* languages.) *Digest* editors work at it as hard, as skillfully, and as artfully as they learned from Wally, and as they, in turn, have passed the technique of condensing on to new generations of editors. Fellow professionals know and admire it greatly, as do article writers and book authors whose work the *Digest* has condensed and carried. Hundreds of letters from these writers and authors to *Digest* editors marvel at "how you retained my style and story, but did it in so many *fewer* words. I, myself, could *not* find where you cut!"

When *Reader's Digest* first became available as a U.S. advertising medium, the three leading general magazines were *LIFE, LOOK,* and *The Saturday Evening Post*—all with extra-large page dimensions. To demonstrate to advertisers that an advertisement designed for those dimensions would work with equal effectiveness in *Digest* dimensions, my creative and art departments made adaptations, and, very often, we condensed the copy. (I chuckle now as I remember a little game I played when warned that the client or agency had said absolutely nothing could be cut. I would condense the copy and have it reset into a clean galley. Then, with a poor-me look on my face, I would plead, "Won't you please read this carefully and tell me what points might be dispensable?" Sometimes I got a sympathetic reading, but more often the galley came tossed back with, "Every point must stay in." That's when I would smile mischievously and say, "Well, then, I'm glad I already condensed it twenty-five percent." And that, most often, would bring an explosive, "B.S.!" and a re-grabbing and intense rereading of the condensed copy. Of course, I had to be very careful doing this, keeping a friendly smile on my face and working hard to ensure we all ended up laughing together. (Thank heaven we most often did.) Thank heaven, too, it was more often a case of advertisers and agencies asking us for help in, as they put it, "shortening the copy without losing anything."

Approach, Procedures, and Techniques

Recall, in Chapter 5, my definition of brevity as a *relative* quality. In this chapter, we will *not* work simply for "short copy." Rather, I will try to help you learn enough about *Digest* condensing to achieve this important advertising objective: **How to say as much in fewer words to make your copy read faster**. (By copy, I mean every word on the page—headlines, subheads, and text.)

Notice, before we go on, the objective above says nothing explicitly about saving space. For example, a 20-word display-type-size subhead might take more space than, say, a 70-word lead paragraph, but it will *make your advertisement read faster*. A picture and caption may communicate much faster than a large number of words alone, but they will take more space than the words. True, we also cut to save space—as when, for example, we must provide enough room to use a copy type size never smaller than 9-point. And this chapter tells how to do that. But because it does, when we get deep into it, you can easily forget— and I don't want you to forget—that our object is saying as *much* in fewer words, *not simply short copy*.

Condensing copy takes far more than applying an editing pencil to cut out words. It requires (1) a particular *approach* to the work, (2) using certain *procedures* (i.e., ways of working), (3) applying proved *techniques* for condensing, and (4) some *artistry*. Of course I cannot teach you—in fact, I cannot even define—the artistry part. Of course, *Digest* editors do the *superb* jobs they do partly because of their artistry. But the foundations of what they do are the *approach*, the *procedures*, and the *techniques*. With those definable, thus *learnable*, skills, anyone willing to study and learn can do satisfactory and useful work.

Approach Before you pick up a pencil, you should have a specific mind-set regarding your objective. While you recognize in advance that, here and there, you may write a few words of "continuity" to connect two parts originally linked by what you have cut, you definitely *do not intend to rewrite everything* (an entirely different job, undertaken only after you have decided, regretfully, that the copy needs complete redoing).

You want to *use what you have*, retaining whatever style, flavor, and so forth it may contain to make the point, to deliver the message, to tell the story, to explain what needs explaining, and to reveal the nuances—in other words, to do *everything* the original copy intended, only *do it in fewer words*. You will have respect for the original, but *ego*—the original writer's or yours—will have no relevance to what you do.

It will help to recall (from Chapter 5) the Index of Comprehension, and how *everything on a page*—layout, typography, illustrations, even colors—can contribute toward moving readers off zero (where they comprehend nothing) toward plus 100 (where they understand everything). So, in editing for ways to make your advertisement read faster, you will look not only at where you can eliminate words, but also examine and consider:

- *Layout:* Can it—and, if so, *does* it—help move readers toward plus 100 and make it easy for them to get there?
- *Content and/or style of any illustrations:* Can they—and, if so, *do* they—help?
- *Predominant colors:* Same questions
- *Headline and art work:* Can they work together better to communicate a message or nuance that otherwise takes many words to get across?
- The possibility of writing a *subhead* that can replace the first copy paragraph or two. Because it will be set in display type and contain many fewer words, this kind of subhead will be faster reading than the original paragraph(s)
- The possibility of using a *picture/caption* in place of many words
- The possibility of using a *table or graph* in place of many words

Procedure Because we now set type so quickly and inexpensively by computer, start your condensing job by having all the copy (including headlines and subheads) *set in the typeface, point size, and pica width in which it will run.* Don't try to work with word-processed copy on $8\frac{1}{2} \times 11$ sheets of paper. When you are condensing to fit a specific space or to allow room for something, "setting to the specs" will show exactly *how much* you need to condense. Also, it provides the quickest, easiest technique for condensing—cutting extreme *widow lines* (covered below).

Read, re-read, and *re-read* the copy until you truly have the gestalt of it all, until you know the pieces, what they say, where they are, and so forth. (In urging this *Digest* technique, an editor wrote, "The best parts will stand up through multiple readings. The weak (and possibly useless) parts will reveal themselves—you will find yourself skipping them.")

Techniques From studying how *Digest* editors do it and from my own years of condensing, I know the following 16 techniques work, and that anyone can learn and apply them.

1. Cut extreme widow lines. Especially when we set copy flush left and right, we will end some paragraphs with extreme widow lines—one or two short words. In cutting copy to provide space for a good, easily readable body type size (or to make room for any other purpose), *lines*, not just words per se, are what you want to eliminate. For copy set, let's say, about 12–13 picas wide, cutting just five one- or two-word widows can "reclaim" as much space as cutting 30 or more words. And I have never seen a paragraph out of which I could not cut a word or two.

You may have been taught to cut widows by working backward "up" the paragraph to change as few lines as possible. That made sense when we set type in hot lead and a change at the *beginning* of a paragraph meant paying to reset the *whole* thing. Now we can delete words anywhere and let the computer rejustify the whole paragraph.

Before we *get* to the technique of cutting redundancy, try this very easy exercise as a "warm-up": Can you spot and cut the redundancy in the following paragraph to bring the widow line "author" up to the third line?

Each volume will be luxuriously bound in premium leather. Embellished with 22-karat gold. And personally hand-signed by its acclaimed author.

2. Don't tell what they already know. Does the copy start "too far back," or *anywhere* in the copy does it tell readers *what they already know?* Immediately suspect words following "as you know" or "needless to say." If they already know or it's needless to say, why say it? The same *sometimes* applies to words after "of course" and "obviously" (though we often properly begin sentences with these words to avoid offending people by implying that *they* don't know what follows).

If you suspect certain words tell "what they already know," ask yourself, "If someone spoke them to me in conversation, and I were in a hurry (as we should always consider potential advertisement readers to be), would those words tempt me to protest, 'Yes, I *know* that, please go on!'" If so, cut those words, and go on.

Using this technique and No. 1 above, and eliminating one redundant word, the *Digest* cut 20 words out of this paragraph, leaving it only three lines long. You do it.

Have you ever wondered how your bank rates you as a credit risk? You know, of course, that it's some combination of facts about your income, your job and so on. But actually, many banks have a scoring system that resembles a school classroom quiz.

3. Cut detours. Edit copy to run in a straight line, each sentence building upon the previous one, each paragraph doing the same. If you have relatively long copy (six column inches or more), outline it to make the detours (i.e., any words that just do not go logically into the outline) stand out for cutting.

When copy does *not* run in a straight A, B, C, D order, it must often double back to remind readers of what it was "saying" before a detour—adding still more unnecessary words. If you ever see words that mean, either literally or in essence, "as we were saying," look back up the copy for a detour—a point where the copy drifted away from the essential message. If the detour does not add something truly important, cut it. If it does, consider boxing it as a separate element.

In A, B, C, D order, a *Digest* article began:

(**A**) *Would you like a larger, more efficient brain? A cure for old age?*

(**B**) *Parentless babies? Body size and skin color to order?*

(**C**) *As a consequence of current discovery and achievement in a number of scientific fields, no ideas about future transformations in the lives of men seem too wild to contemplate.*

(**D**) *In sober, scientific circles today, there is no doubt that man will acquire control of his own heredity and evolution. And the discussion seldom leaves much doubt that man will acquire this control. It's a question of when, not if.*

(**E**) *All of which means that brain-wracking complexities— legal, social, ethical, moral, philosophical, religious—are soon to be thrust upon us.*

Those 112 words flow in a logical straight-line sequence. But the *Digest* cut something over 200 words between and around them because the sequence in which the content of those points (not the actual "lead-in, lead-out" words that *Digest* editors used for *their* sequence) originally appeared was (E), (B), (C), (A), and (D)!

4. Edit for active voice. You cannot change *all* sentences to the active voice. And you don't ever want to warp your word structure simply to use transitive verbs. Better to leave in a smoothly fitting "is" or "was." But, within reason, consider it a victory when you can edit most of the copy to the active voice. For this not only reduces the number of words, but also produces more vigorous, more rhythmic copy:

A fat man is loved by everyone. *(Passive, 7 words.)*
Everyone loves a fat man. *(Active, 5 words, more punch, more rhythm.)*

The following 26-word paragraph started the copy of an automotive advertisement. By editing to the active voice, condense it to about 20 words—and, in the process, make it more forceful, more rhythmic:

When technology and craftsmanship are meticulously combined, and when form is blended flawlessly with function, a utilitarian object becomes an example of the art of design.

5. Don't labor the point. When you must document a point, don't throw in every piece of documentation simply because you have it. When you must give an example, *one* might do it. If you must demonstrate that something applies in several different ways, two, or at most three *(short ones)*, demonstrations will do.

By eliminating excess documentation (and using any other technique we have covered this far), condense this advertising paragraph of over 70 words to about 35 or 40:

They are the most celebrated authors on this globe of earth. Their books have been read by millions of people throughout the world. When they have new books published, the books consistently become best sellers, and libraries have long waiting lists of people eager to get and read them. But, until now, only the privileged have been able to acquire the modern masterpieces of our greatest authors in prized first editions.

6. Repetition, OK; redundancy, no. In advertising copy—so often skim-read with minds elsewhere—we occasionally need *some* repetition. But because advertising copy tends to get "exuberant," redundancy often makes it run longer than necessary. I suspect the following sentence would "get by" most readings. But, with our eyes now looking for redundancy, what words stand out for cutting?

Nutritious, vitamin-and-mineral-packed XXXXX Bran Flakes provide the bulk and roughage your body needs.

And what five words can you cut from this without losing one iota of content?

Precisely accurate, beautifully stylish, economically low-priced, our brand new XXXXX is everything we first started out to make it.

In advertising, we commonly start the copy by repeating the headline, either word for word or in essence. Sometimes, that's OK, but always look at such repetition critically. In the following, which words should remain as helpful advertising repetition and which should go as just plain redundant?

At your Sprintor dealer now!

**The All-New
4-Wheel Drive
Sprintor Wagon**

They're in! The all-new 4-wheel drive Sprintor Wagons.

They bring the first truly significant advance in automotive

drive trains since automatic transmission. The all-new 4-

wheel drive Sprintor Wagon. At your Sprintor dealer now.

Or suppose your copy includes this headline, subhead, and first paragraph. If you look for redundancy, you have two possible cuts, one of 20 words or another of 24:

**MicroRave®
Cherry Pie
Good as Mom
Ever Made**

**Real home-made flavor and texture
in just five minutes...with new
MicroRave Cherry Pie and
MicroRave Instant Pie Crust.**

Your family will love the home-made flavor and texture of

MicroRave Cherry Pie, and you can microwave-bake one

in only five minutes. From starting to bake to setting a

beautiful steaming cherry pie aside to cool, it takes only

five minutes! Just open the box, etc., etc.

7. Edit for positive/negative pairs. Because of advertising's tendency to repeat and labor a point, we sometimes say the same thing in both positive and negative form. (It's not difficult, it's easy!) We may do it for emphasis, but we should look suspiciously at such pairs, and, unless they pass the "emphasis" test, cut one part (preferably the negative). When *Digest* editors applied the test to the following positive/negative pair, they cut eight words. Can you see how they did it?

> *The answer does not rest with carelessness or incompetence. It lies largely in a great mystery surrounding most mental retardation.*

If you do, then cut about as much out of this advertising copy.

> *On cold winter nights, you don't want to turn the key and hear nothing but a weak whine from your car engine. You can rest assured that when you turn the key, you will hear your car engine varoom with power.*

8. Tighten it up. Look for loosely connected sentences that can be combined or otherwise tightened up. CLUES: Often, such sentences read with a sing-song monotony. Equally often, they do because of the intransitive verbs in them, the passive voice of it all. Hence, one technique for tightening up loosely connected sentences involves changing intransitive verbs to transitive, editing from passive to active voice.

Apply this technique to the following made-up advertising copy, and, if you do it as I did, you will end up with a net cut (you add a few to subtract many) of about 18 words and make it read much better, too:

> *For the second year in a row, XXXXX has been voted the Car of the Year. The judges for this prestigious honor are selected members of the International Association of Automotive Engineers and the editors of Motortime News. XXXXX was cited by these automotive experts for "overall excellence." And its overhead cam, fuel injection V-6 engine was rated as the "epitome of internal combustion engine design."*

9. Bring subject and verb together. When you see the subject of a sentence separated from the principal verb by a phrase or clause, try to bring the subject and verb together by moving the phrase or clause to the beginning of the sentence. This technique often cuts words because you do not then have to name the subject twice—once as a noun, and again as a pronoun. Using this technique, you can cut five words from **A dog, if you fail to discipline him, becomes a household pest** (12 words). You do it by making the sentence read **An undisciplined dog becomes a household pest** (7 words).

The condensations of these advertising sentences use the same technique:

Canned soup, unless it was cooked with salt, simply would not taste good. (13)

Unless cooked with salt, canned soup simply would not taste good. (11)

Or: **Cooked without salt, canned soup simply would not taste good.** (10)

Even the best-made furniture, when you expose it for years to hot-air heat, will eventually come loose at the rungs. (22)

Exposed for years to hot-air heat, even the best-made furniture will eventually come loose at the rungs. (19)

10. Eliminate commonly used words you don't need. One of the most common such words is *not* in this subhead—the word "that." When I write, especially rapidly, I'm as guilty as anyone of over-using it. Yet, when reminded, I know as well as anyone "he knew *that* he could do it" can go as "he knew he could do it"; or "the bread *that* kids love" runs one word shorter as "the bread kids love." When you need only delete a word or two to cut a widow and save a line, look for other commonly used unnecessary words such as *case, character, who is* (or *was*), *which is* (or *was*), as in the following examples:

We have very few cases of dissatisfied customers. (8)	We have very few dissatisfied customers. (6)
products of superior character (4)	superior products (2)
Our service manager, who is specially trained . . . (7)	Our service manager, specially trained . . . (5) OR: Our specially trained service manager . . . (5)
Our bread, which is always made . . . (6)	Our bread, always made . . . (4)

11. Eliminate commonly used *groups* of unnecessary words. These often take the form of trite groups of words for which you can substitute one word, or at least fewer words. Because we see them so often, such phrases easily slip by unnoticed unless we make ourselves sensitive to them.

The question as to whether ...	whether
There is no doubt that ...	no doubt OR doubtlessly
In the interest of economy ...	for economy
He is a man who ...	he
In a hasty manner	hastily ·
This is a subject that ...	this subject

In all writing, including advertising copy, we often see—and should jump when we see—the words "*the fact that.*" They are usually useless and often carry unnecessary "supporting" words with them.

owing to the fact that	since OR because
in spite of the fact that	although OR though
Because of the fact that we introduced this product ...	Because we introduced this product ...

12. Look for qualifiers. Sometimes in advertising, for legal reasons or for nuances of meaning, we *must* use qualifiers. But copywriters often do because they feel qualifiers add a "laid-back" tone to their writing or make the copy more "conversational." Nothing wrong with these objectives; but qualifiers not required for legality or precision can be cut quickly and easily (e.g., the italicized qualifying words in these phrases: "*rather* nice," "*awfully* good," "*quite* appetizing," "*frightfully* expensive").

13. Make it positive. The positive form of expression always rates over the negative, especially in advertising. And changing from negative to positive will often eliminate words. Sometimes, it also will change an intransitive verb to transitive—another advantage. A *Digest* editorial memo gave these examples:

| He was not often late in arriving. (7—intrans.) | He rarely arrived late. (4—trans.) |
| He did not think that studying Latin was a very sensible way to use one's time. (16—intrans.) | He considered studying Latin a waste of time. (8—trans.) |

Using the same technique, try condensing these pieces of copy:

> With XXXX Frozen Dinners, you will not go without the nutrition you still need when "baching" it.
>
> The XXXX Toothbrush keeps you from missing those crevices where plaque forms and builds.

14. Watch the anecdotes. We see many anecdotes in articles but hardly any in advertisements. Perhaps we should see more—they do make good reading, and, if selected and written skillfully, they can make a point with unique fullness because they "illustrate" it. They do, however, require more words than straight exposition.

So, if you ever find anecdotal words in advertising copy, decide if they provide the most effective, efficient way to make the point. If you decide "yes," remember that when we "tell a story," we can (1) easily ramble on too long and/or (2) include details not relevant to the reason for including the anecdote. (Have you ever suffered listening to someone including so many irrelevant details you felt like urging, "For heaven's sake, get to the point!"?) Think that way when considering anecdotal advertising copy. Keep it short and keep it all relevant.

15. BF lead-ins save lines. Recall that when condensing copy in type we cut words to cut *lines*. And, though we surely don't want solidly packed, all gray columns of copy, which discourage reading and make it harder to read, we often don't need to waste all the lines it takes to run centered copy subheads. We can retain most of the advantages of copy subheads without using so many lines by using boldface lead-ins instead.

(last line of paragraph)	(last line of paragraph)
(space)	(space)
(**BF Centered Subhead**)	(**BF Lead-in**)(first line next paragraph.)
(space)	
(first line of next paragraph)	

16. When finished, STOP. In advertising, we have a tendency to want to "get in a few more words" or "another urging." Often, the few more words add nothing. If, after people have read your copy, they don't accept your proposition, a few more words won't help. Especially such vacuous sentences as "Your family will thank you" or "We worked hard to make it easy for you." And the typical "another urging" generally comes off as a gratuitous and even sometimes laughingly impractical plea: "Go to your local XXXX dealer (or pick up a can of XXXX) today"—read at 11:30 P.M. or on Sunday; "Hurry! Call your aluminum gutter contractor..." when readers would not hurry even if they *knew where to find* such a contractor. I *know* such "dealer" lines often must run as dealer sops, but always look suspiciously at the last few words or lines. If the ending copy no longer contains anything of value, and thus of interest, to readers, and if it need not be there for some marketing or legal reasons, CUT!

Typography: The Voice of Print

10

I include this chapter primarily for the surprising number of people in advertising who have never given typography much, if *any*, thought, and who don't know (and have not, till now, had anyone suggest that they *should* know) even the basics. I include it primarily for those who approach this chapter with the three questions I know enter the minds of nearly all with whom I start a seminar on typography:

1. Why should I bother to learn *anything* about typography?
2. If I *do* need to learn a few things, what's worth my knowing?
3. If I take time to learn these few things, what can I *do* with that knowledge?

Why Learn Anything?

Suppose you were previewing a television commercial, and the producer said, "Wait till you hear the *character* in this voice-over—it's better than Orson Welles!" But then the voice sounded like the guy had loose dentures—you couldn't understand a word. What would you say? Of course: "We'd better forget the character and get some *clarity*." You *know* a TV voice-over must come through so clearly that people will hear and understand it even when talking to someone and not really watching—when they either say, "Wait a minute, I want to see this," or keep right on talking. Elementary, right? Or suppose you had a product calling for soft, subtle sex appeal in the script, and the voice was as shrill as we remember Phyllis Diller's? You would think the people who made the commercial were playing a damned expensive joke.

For broadcast commercials, you know that voices can be very easy or very *difficult* to hear and/or understand. You know that voices can add emotion—*flavor*—to commercials and that they can add the right or the *wrong* feeling.

Well, as the title of this chapter says, think of typography as what it is: *The Voice of Print!* And recognize that typography, too, can be very easy or very *difficult* to read and/or "understand." That typography, too, can add emotion—flavor—to print advertisements and that it can add the right or the *wrong* feeling.

But very, very few in advertising know enough—or even *think* enough—about typography to take such positions. Very, very few (and I'm sorry, but forced, to include art directors*) have it so clearly and firmly in mind that they never forget the cardinal rule for typography in advertising: **The primary objective of typography in advertising, the objective overriding all others, is easy—EASY— readability.**

David Ogilvy: "You may think I exaggerate the importance of good typography. But do you think an advertisement can sell if nobody can read it?"

I will say it as many times as it takes to embed it in as many minds as I can reach: The typography in our advertisements must *always* be so easy to read (with one rare exception**) that people start reading before they decide to and, if the material interests them, continue reading with absolutely no effort. This must be true because of the advertising truth: **All other things being equal, the *easier* an advertisement is to read, the *more likely* it will be read; the *more difficult*, the *less likely*.**

More Honored in the Breach If everyone knew, and never forgot, that the primary objective of typography in advertising is easy—EASY—readability, we would never see headlines that, like the one at left, are nearly impossible to read, and absolutely impossible to scan-read:

THINKING
BIG
IN THE SPACE AGE

*With notable exceptions (e.g., Louellen Jones of Rubin Postaer, which, not coincidentally, is a great agency for print advertising).
**The one rare exception: When, for a special illustrative reason, we *deliberately* make the headline a bit difficult to read; but people instantly understand *why* and will go along with it.

We would never see a headline obviously set not for easy readability but to fit someone's idea of fashion—or something—as was the headline from which I modeled the example at right.

Or, note just below that: We would never see type mixed, line-broken, and set this way, simply because someone felt it made the headline lively, I guess, and/or exciting. Forgetting—or perhaps never knowing—that while type-faces can enhance the meaning of words, if people glance and do not easily read anything meaningful, you have no liveliness, no excitement.

We would never have seen and would never see again that awful—and awfully unwise—fad that has for some years now dictated how fad-followers must set a so-called modern advertisement headline: Condensed sans serif bold or ultrabold, set all caps (or, as here, for variety I suppose, caps and not very small caps), and, as a *coup de grace* to readability, set either solid or near solid. (I feel compelled to rewrite this headline, **TO MAKE YOUR WRITING MORE RIVETING, STOP MAKING IT HARD TO READ**.)

If everyone knew, and never forgot, that the primary objective of typography in advertising is easy—EASY—readability, we would never see blocks of copy set in a sans serif italic and at angles—both entirely for design, not for easy reading:

If we all hewed to the primary objective, we would need an extraordinarily strong overriding reason to *not* work by this truth:

> A Traditional Serif Face,
> Set Upper and Lower Case Roman,
> Makes The Most Easily Readable
> Headline and Body Copy.

Of course, I don't mean that specific face (New Century Schoolbook). I mean that easily readable. But, oh, I can hear the wails: "Thaaat would make everything look alike! It would be boooorrrring!" Before you join in the wailing chorus, consider this:

ALL CAPS SANS SERIF BOLD OR ULTRA BOLD, SET SOLID, CONDENSED AND IN SEVERAL DECKS, MAKING HEADLINES BOTH NOTICEABLE AND VERY DIFFICULT TO READ, HAS ITSELF BECOME BORING.

Later in this chapter, we will look deeper into the use of typefaces and settings for readability and special effects. But, for now, I hope what you have read and seen thus far has *started* to answer the question of "why bother to learn anything about typography?" So we can move on to the second question.

What's Worth Your Knowing?

Of course expert specification of type for easiest readability and most imaginative use of typography to enhance the flavor and/or impact of your message demand considerable knowledge and talent. *But,* with (1) unwavering adherence to that primary objective of readability above all, (2) continually remembering that you *can* enhance communication of flavor through typography, plus (3) the relatively few meat-and-potato facts and truths coming up next, *anyone* can participate in creating typographically great advertising.

The Three Families
of Typefaces

Especially since we have added all the computer-set type-faces, we have hundreds from which to select. But they all fall into one of three families.

Serif Faces These include all faces with definitive endings (serifs) to the open-ended letter strokes and most corners of letters. (Serifs are circled.) Serifs finish off the lines and corners, and do it with variations on three basic designs, which I will describe and illustrate.

For example, consider Goudy, which has rounded serifs (note how they curve gracefully from the stems and corners of the letters). Such rounded serifs produce THE easiest-reading style of serif face, which makes rounded serif fonts the easiest to read typefaces of *all*. I don't mean Goudy specifically and alone. I mean typefaces with rounded serifs.

This is Bodoni, a thin, straight-line serif face designed by an Italian named Giambattista Bodoni for a specific reason. But, because few know what he had in mind, we often see this face misused. Notice that the serifs make very thin, sharp lines and that the thick strokes of each letter connect to very thin lines.

Back in Bodoni's working days—in the mid 1700s—all paper was uncoated and soft. Printing ink blotted—spread out from the letter lines—as drawn (slightly exaggerated) at top. Ink does not do this on the hard, coated paper of today, as drawn at bottom.

This is Goudy.
A round serif face.

This is Bodoni.
A line serif face.

This is how Bodoni appears
on a coated stock

**This is how Bodoni
appears on a soft stock**

That's why Bodoni, when printed on today's coated paper, comes off a bit too "contrasty," and thus a bit less readable than other serif faces (note top). But when printed on un-coated, soft paper, *as Bodoni designed it to be*, the thin lines thicken, the contrast diminishes, and it turns beautifully easy to read. (But note this *negative* point: The extremely thin lines, deliberately so designed as just explained, make Bodoni a poor face to set in reverse. It's too easy for the thin lines to "fill in.")

In addition to rounded and straight-line serifs, we have block serifs such as this face, Memphis. It's good for school varsity letters, and for special effects with a *few* headline words, but not for much else—not for a long headline, and absolutely not for body copy. Readers would stumble over those bulky block serifs.

This is Memphis Roman.
A block serif face.

Faces such as Serif Gothic are what I call "semi serifs"—not quite a serif face and not quite a stick letter. As I view most compromises, I see it as a nothing face—antiseptic—with serifs too weak to hold your eyes on the line and adding little to the character of the letters. This is very much like a face called Copperplate Gothic, which (I remember from my days as a bank advertising manager) was the "required" face for the year-end statement-of-assets tombstone advertisements that all banks ran. That surely says something about its sterility.

This is Serif Gothic.
Not quite a serif face
and not quite a sans serif.

Yet, for a period in the too-often-played advertising game of lemmings-follow-the-lemmings, Serif Gothic became the hot face. Everywhere you looked, you saw it used for both headline and body copy. And that's something you should watch for and avoid: Fads in advertising typography. Note the typography of advertisements other than your own so you will know whether you're using a face because it's right for your advertisement or simply because it's the current rage.

In addition to variations in serif treatment, all serif faces have, as part of their designs, contrasts between "thicks" and "thins"—some strokes of the letters being thick and some thin. The range of contrast runs from extreme (top) through medium (center) to hardly noticeable (bottom).

ABW

ABW

ABW

Stroke thickness is one of the variables type designers use in creating typefaces. But to you, the amount of contrast between thicks and thins is one factor that determines whether blocks of your copy have, for example, a calm or a staccato "look" and whether your copy blocks appear gray and flat or bold with good contrast (called the "color" of the type).

Rarely in advertising, especially when you want to run a headline in reverse, should you use a face with extreme contrast between thicks and thins. Nor, however, do I recommend a face with very *little* contrast between thicks and thins except when you absolutely must run a copy block in reverse—it comes off as too "chunky." Almost always, — as with so many things in typography (and life), moderation makes the best rule. Almost always go with a medium contrast between thick and thins.

Sans Serif Faces The second family of typefaces (both in order in this book and, I think, in terms of how much of it should be used in advertising) are the *sans* (without) serifs—stick lettering, the way lettering started. It certainly has its uses in advertising, and I would use nothing else for such single words as **NEW** and **FREE**. (I cannot resist the facetious addition that it also works perfectly on doors, for the words **MEN** and **WOMEN**.)

This is Helvetica.
A sans serif face.

Helvetica provides a good illustration of sans serif in more ways than one. It is a pure sans serif, and it (along with Futura, Frutiger, Universe and other nice, open, round, and flowing faces) offers one of the most legible sans serifs. And I have no problem with using such faces for some headlines and even some small pieces of body copy.

I think none of us in the "serif camp" would argue so strongly against sans serif in advertising, particularly for body copy, if so many of today's art directors didn't argue *for* it for what we consider the wrong reasons. And if they didn't misuse it. They call it clean and uncluttered— no argument there—though they fail to see that clean and uncluttered also makes it sterile and cold. On top of that, they ignore all the research that has proved many times over many years that, in reading ease and degree of comprehension, serif faces rank greatly superior to sans serifs. I have never, *never*, seen any research disputing, for example, such findings as Colin Wheildon's most recent (purposely set in sans serif below to demonstrate one of its good uses, for charts and tables):

	Comprehension Levels		
	Good	**Fair**	**Poor**
Body copy set in sans serif	22	37	41
Body copy set in serif	83	9	8

The sans serif advocates argue that, given enough time, people will have less and less difficulty with sans serif as they become more and more used to seeing and reading it. To which I (and all advertisers should) respond: I'm not in business to accustom people to like and read sans serif. I want the most easily read advertisements I can get *now*, and if that means using mainly serif faces because that's where people are, who dares to disagree? I think only the typographically uneducated would argue, and the *arrogantly* uneducated at that.

Specialty Faces I smile as I write about and prepare to show this third family of typefaces—the happy costume-ballers. While neither I nor any sensible typographer would use them except with great caution and sparingly, they do, indeed, add much color, flavor, and variety to typography. (I imagine it's great fun to design them.)

Because we set type photographically now, we can achieve much finer and fancier lines, thus more—and more elaborate—specialty faces than ever. Specialty faces come in two forms as shown below:

Many, Many Specialty Faces

ABRAMESQUE

BOBO BOLD

CALYPSO

Darling Bossy

Fat Albert Shadow

GALLIA

MOORE LIBERTY

And Special Cuttings of regular faces

Baskerville Hunt Special

Bodoni Open

Caslon 471 Roman

CHELTENHAM shadow

Goudy Mediaeval

Helvetica Flair

Melior Bold Outline

As you can see, we have true specialty faces, designed originally to be what they are, and we have special designs of otherwise *regular* faces. We have no regular faces called Abramesque or (I love the name) Fat Albert Shadow. But notice one up from the bottom of the column at right— our plain Helvetica elegantly costumed as Helvetica Flair. And Baskerville, Bodoni, Caslon, Cheltenham, Goudy—all traditional faces that go way back—are shown here fancied up for specialty use.

Also because we set type photographically now, we can do special effects with both regular and specialty faces. We can actually use type as an illustrative graphic. Here you see it soft as a hedge and hard as steel. We can make it look frozen, melting, or steaming; you name the condition. We can display it at an angle, flip it, twist it, squash it—do just about anything you want. Which is, of course, both wonderful and dangerous. I get apprehensive thinking about such power at the disposal of those who don't know enough to adhere even to the fundamentals of the discipline.

On the other hand, I think the "law-abiding" people in advertising could do more with special effects than I see now. They could communicate through such special effects as well as through word meaning and picture content, as we do when we use different tones of voice and inflections for the same words.

Basics of Setting

Different ways of setting type add to the variety provided by the different typefaces themselves. As just noted, we can now do extraordinary things. The following, however, continues with the meat-and-potatoes menu of the basics.

All the regular faces, but not all of the specialty faces, can be set "roman," a term sometimes mistakenly used to mean a typeface with serifs. It means straight up and down, in *either* serif or sans serif. You are reading type set "roman" right now. You also can set all regular faces and a few specialty faces in "*italic*," as that word is set. The letters slant a bit like handwriting, which is why it is sometimes mistakenly called "script" (a style of typeface—a specialty face—not a setting).

Then you have a choice of typeface thickness or "weight." From, as you see here, "light" through "regular" through "demibold" (which means semibold) to "bold" and "ultra bold." There is also another weight called "hairline," which is thinner than even that sans serif word "Light." Hairline comes as a sans-serif only; I've never heard of a hairline serif face.

Light	Light
Regular	Regular
Demi-Bold	Demi-Bold
Bold	**Bold**
Ultra-Bold	**Ultra-Bold**

Next comes a cross between type *styles* and type *settings*. This has to do with the widths of the letters. Some type designs simply have wide letters; some have "normal" and

abcdefghijklmnopqrstuvwxyz

abcdefghijklmnopqrstuvwxyz

some narrow letters. But we have available to us different "cuttings" of the *same* faces, some that set, as I call it, "open and round" and some that set compacted:

Also, we can set many typefaces CONDENSED, REG-ULAR, or EXPANDED. And, with the new computerized setting of type, we can now set the letters so close together they touch each other or, as we always could, set the letters with space between them, in which case they are called "letter spaced."

This is the same size CONDENSED

This is the same size REGULAR

This is the same size EXPANDED

set touching: Typography
very tight: Typography
tight: Typography
normal: Typography
or letter spaced: Typography

In setting type, we can, of course, choose different sizes, which we measure in "points," 72 points to the inch.

This is 6-point, which you should never use except for legal copy.

This is 72-pt.

Above 72 points, we measure in inches—sizes you will generally use only in large newspaper advertisements and, of course, on billboards. To make a fact about point size clear, I have saved this illustration for here although it really belongs with the discussion of type design.

All letters have bodies, the part in the center of any line you read. Some letters have ascenders, strokes that rise above the center area, and some letters have descenders, which drop below the center area. Although point size was originally taken from the size of the piece of metal on which

the letter sat, for our purposes we can measure point size from the top of the highest ascender to the bottom of the lowest descender. This will come into play when we deal with using type, as will the fact, illustrated here, that ascenders and descenders vary in length for different typefaces.

bpf   bpf   bpf

short   medium   long

bpf   bpf   **bpf**

You have another choice in setting type: The width (or length) of the lines, measured in "picas," of which there are six to the inch. The lines in *Reader's Digest* run $12\frac{1}{2}$ picas wide ($2\frac{1}{16}$ inches). Newspaper columns range from 10 to 12 picas; the lines of a paperback book run about 25 picas, and those of a hardback are from 25 to 35 picas wide, depending on the size of the book.

The final choice in setting type is leading—how close together or far apart you space the lines.

LEADED:

With spaces
between lines

SOLID:

No spaces
between lines

With lines set upper and lower case (u&lc), because of the ascenders and descenders, you will always have *some* space between the letter bodies even if you "set solid" (without leading). But there will be no space between the lowest descenders and the highest ascenders of the line below. When you use leading, you *do* have spaces between them.

What
You Can Do
with What You Now Know

What you have read and seen in this chapter represents only what I think it will *help* you to know about typography. That basic knowledge, plus the guidelines for using it are given and illustrated in the remainder of this chapter.

First I will give you guidelines to help assure that your advertisements always meet the primary objective (remember, overriding all others) of typography in advertising: Easy—EASY—readability. After that will come suggestions for taking advantage of the opportunities provided by typography to occasionally add flavor, strength, and/or extra interest to your advertisements.

Always Meeting the Primary Objective From now on, when you look at layouts, pay close attention to (1) the typeface or faces selected and (2) how they are set or specified to be set.

About the headline, remember we want a typeface and setting that makes it so easy to read people will do so just by glancing at it. And we want body copy so easy to read they can do so AND comprehend what they read even if they simply scan-read (not "they can read it if they try," but they will read it *without* trying). Typeface selection and setting (plus layout) determine readability. Here is a general guide to the most easily readable faces and settings:

- **Typefaces with rounded serifs (which means, of course, not sans serif).**
- **Faces with short- to medium-length ascenders and descenders.**
- **Faces with medium contrast between thick and thin lines.**
- **Set u&lc roman.**
- **Set bold to semibold (sometimes ultrabold) for headlines and regular to bold for body copy.**
- **Body copy never smaller than 9-point (of a face with medium-length ascenders and descenders).**

Please don't tell anyone—especially if you're a client, don't tell your agency—that Tony Antin says the only readable faces and settings are those above. I say that those guidelines produce THE *most* easily readable headlines and copy. But I say also that there are other very readable settings that may not meet one or two of those specifications (*except* the "must" of body copy no smaller than 9 point). And, as noted earlier, when you can greatly help your advertisement with some typographic special effect, you may deliberately trade off a *small* degree of readability. But, as I also noted earlier, THE *most* easily readable faces and settings are the *least noticed* faces and settings.

Restrictions for Sans Serif in Headlines Avoid ultrabold, except for a single word or two. Ditto for all caps. Never set solid. Never set with lines artificially broken to form some pattern like this:

**A SANS SERIF
WHEN SET ALL CAPS
BOLD AND CONDENSED,
ESPECIALLY WHEN SET TO
FIT SOME PATTERN INSTEAD
OF WITH LINE BREAKS AS
THE WORDS MIGHT BE
SPOKEN MAKES NO
SENSE AT ALL**

Enter Dynamic Headlines We go for those predetermined patterns because of something we commonly do with headlines: When we stack the lines, we feel we must center each line exactly in the middle of the page, like a see-saw board. And we feel we must arrange the lines to fit some newspaper headline pattern—flush left and right, pyramid or inverted pyramid, flush left random right, perfectly staggered, and so on. We strive for a design, with little or no thought about how the lines break and read. So we end up with headlines as at right.

The Xxxxxxxx "Win an Ice Cream Wagon" Sweepstakes

If, while absentmindedly turning pages, I just glanced at that, I might wonder how one wins "an ice." Or get no meaning from the words "Cream Wagon."

For some years now, I have been preaching a new approach. I call it Dynamic Headlining, and the best way to explain is to demonstrate:

Dynamic Headline:
    Stack and break lines
for easy reading in visual gulps
      and to make your key words stand out;
and if you can make
          the words work
      synergistically
          with the illustrations,
                that's a plus.

And that, of course, is a bit of an exaggeration to emphasize the point that I don't care about the exterior shape of the headline as long as it doesn't end up looking like it's about to tip over. In that case I would have to do something purely cosmetic about it. But what I'm after is (1) a headline that reads as easy as falling down stairs, (2) one that works hand-in-glove with my illustrations, and, (3) one in which my key words stand out.

In Dynamic Headlining, you tend to break your headline into short vertical "takes," which makes sense for easy reading. You can read the same number of words faster when they are broken that way than when they are set all on one long line because your eyes see and read two or three such short lines at the same time.

Look at this fine demonstration of Dynamic Headlining from *Reader's Digest*. Note how easily your eyes flow down the one-word lines and how the words work so synergistically with the art.

And, going totally Dynamic, Brach's used the technique not only for the headline but also for all the copy. Your eyes move effortlessly down the copy, and the candy illustrations work with the words every step of the way:

Edgar
Bergen's
Final
Farewell

With permission of E. J. Brach Corp.

The opposite of a Dynamic Headline is what I call a Static Headline, and again the best way to explain is to demonstrate:

Static Headline: Break and stack lines to center them for perfect artificial see-saw balance and some predetermined exterior shape; often burying key words, breaking lines in all the wrong places; with your art seeming to sit there, unrelated to the head.

That, too, is a bit exaggerated to dramatize how, for the sake of centering lines and making the headline fit a pre-determined (for no good reason) shape, we break lines between words that belong together (e.g., "to" and "center," "see-saw" and "balance," "exterior" and "shape"). The whole thing sits there rigid, static, and as visually dead as an inscription on a tombstone.

Many art directors consider the BMW headline style hot stuff, and I really incurred the wrath of some in the audience when I criticized a headline set and stacked this way: I contend that, set in the difficult-to-speed-read all-caps sans serif, with the lines centered and broken that way, you cannot quickly/easily scan-read and grasp the two important copy points: "worth more used" and "worth more new."

MAYBE A BMW IS WORTH MORE USED BECAUSE IT'S WORTH MORE NEW

One art director said, "That typeface and setting is the arrogant voice of BMW." Others contended that the face and setting created a macho flavor (apparently forgetting all the women who lovingly drive their Beamers). They were so centered on the "flavor," that I could not resist (even at the risk of bodily assault) suggesting that, if the words meant nil to them and flavor was all, why not make the headline read as at right.

I admit that was both tactless and not too smart. I got in my shot, but I so antagonized them they were not even listening or looking when I made what I think was an intelligent suggestion: If they truly felt that a BMW advertisement needed a bold sans serif for a macho flavor in its headlines, they could keep what they used, only set it in the more easily readable u&lc and also set a Dynamic Headline as shown at right.

VAROOM! VAROOM! VAROOM! VAROOM! VAROOM! VAROOM! VAROOM! VAROOM! VAROOM!

Maybe a BMW is worth more <u>used</u> because it is worth more <u>new.</u>

U&lc vs. ALL CAPS I hope by now you have concluded that u&lc makes the most easily readable setting. If you have any doubt, take a look at these figures from another of Colin Wheildon's recent tests:

Legibility of Headline Styles:
Serif upper and lower case **92%**
Sans serif upper and lower case **90%**
BLACK LETTER ALL CAPS **3%**

If you're still not totally convinced that u&lc beats all caps all hollow for readability, I'll give you even more proof. Starting with the results of another Wheildon test:

	Comprehension Level	
	ALL CAPS	Upper and Lower Case
Serif Face	**69**	**92**
Sans Serif	57	90

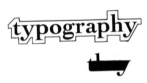

Words set in lower case, because of the ascenders and descenders, form distinctive shapes, and part of reading is recognizing these distinctive silhouettes. For years, I have asked audiences what they get out of that black shape under the word "typography" at left, and always and immediately comes the chorus "they."

I believe Miles A. Tinker, University of Minnesota psychologist, first did this experiment to demonstrate that the upper halves of printed lines furnish more clues to those word silhouettes that help us read than the lower halves do. I use a variation of it to demonstrate that we get "upper half help" when we set copy u&lc, but do not get it when we set it all caps.

The fact that you can read
this copy shows how much we
depend on the outline of words
especially the upper half

First I show what you see now, ask who will stand and read it, and see practically all hands go up. Someone does, in fact, read it easily—as I'm sure you already have.

WHEN YOU SET COPY ALL CAPS

YOU DO NOT HAVE DISTINCTIVE

UPPER HALF WORD OUTLINES

THAT'S ONE REASON WHY IT IS

NOT SO EASY TO READ

Then I show this copy, also with the bottom half whited out, but set in all caps. Now rarely, if ever, does a hand go up. And when someone finally tries it, he or she struggles, and hardly anyone gets through it correctly.

Again, I beg you, please don't oversimplify what I say. I don't say that all-caps setting is *never* any good. I have already noted that, for certain words and/or in certain contexts, I would use nothing else. I say simply and strongly and without reservation that typography for advertising must make for the easiest readability, and for headlines and, most emphatically, for copy, to achieve that objective, set u&lc.

Headline Size Guide I noted earlier that because of our experience with newspapers, we tend to equate size of headline with importance of news. A trick of the trade I have learned from experience is to determine the size your sense of proportion says the headline *should* be for the dimensions of the advertisement, then *bump it up* from about four to ten points, depending on the size of the advertisement. I don't mean elephantine, but I do mean somewhat jumbo. To eyes sensitive to perfect proportions, it will appear a bit too big. However, no *reader* will say (or think) that, but he or she will somehow feel an extra pull to the headline.

But, note this, *impression* of size makes more difference than actual point size. The right size to make a headline "somewhat jumbo" depends on (1) the size of the advertisement, (2) the dimensions of the publication in which it appears, (3) the weight of the type (light, regular, demibold, etc.), (4) the way the lines are broken and stacked and the resulting number of lines, (5) their placement on the page(s), and (6) the lengths of the ascenders and descenders. (I'll explain why when we get to body copy below.) A lot of variables there. Too many for me to give you a definitive-for-all-cases headline size guide. But I don't feel helpful enough leaving you with that, so I'll venture at least this much:

- Ignoring truly small space units (e.g., one column, four inches), thinking the "smallest" unit to be a half-page in *Reader's Digest, TV Guide,* or *Prevention,* forget type smaller than 24 points. And for a full size newspaper spread, I know you will never get too *big.* The "errors" I see almost always fall on the too small side because far more art directors have an "artist" as opposed to a "communicator" orientation. I don't call that good or bad; I simply offer it as a reason. But they don't seem to have any problem with making the sound of a broadcast commercial a bit too loud, so they shouldn't hesitate to make the headline "a bit too big."
- If, after going through the exercise of selecting what might appear proportionate and then bumping it up, you must for some strong reason go smaller again, go **bolder**. Rarely, and only if you have some special reason, go to ultrabold. Go instead to one of the new computer weights called "black" or to the old demibold or bold.
- If you run a headline in one long line (as opposed to breaking it into short lines), you not only make it harder to read, but also reduce the impression of size, especially if you place it high across the very top of the page or pages. Don't do that.

Body Copy Size Guide For body copy that you want *all* readers to be able to scan-read easily, never go smaller than 9-point (of a face with short to medium ascenders/descenders); and use 10- to 14-point type (or even a bit larger) if you can. In a large newspaper advertisement, use 18-point at least.

After 36 years of working with advertisements in *Digest* dimensions, I can say this and challenge anyone to prove me wrong: I have never seen an advertisement for which I couldn't get in *all* the essential points using at least 9-point type—and in a pleasant flowing writing style—neither staccato nor with fragmented sentences.

Effects of Ascenders/Descenders Recall that different type faces have different-length ascenders and descenders, ranging from short to medium to long. Recall also that we can measure type size from the top of the highest ascender to the bottom of the lowest descender. Further, recall that the ascenders and descenders come up or go down from the letter bodies. All this means that the longer the ascenders and descenders are, the smaller the letter bodies will be and vice versa. For example, setting 12-point, if the ascenders and descenders each use 3 points, that leaves only 6 points for the bodies. If the ascenders and descenders each use only 2 points, that leaves 8 points for the bodies. This has a significant effect on how large or small any point size looks, and, especially in body copy, on ease or difficulty of reading:

This typeface is Bookman, a face with relatively short ascenders and descenders, set 12 point regular. Note that the bodies are larger than Berkeley's; that it actually seems to be a larger point size.

This typeface is Berkeley, a face with relatively long ascenders and descenders, set 12 point regular. Note that the letter bodies are smaller than those of Bookman; that it actually seems to be a smaller point size.

Thus, I recommend that when you use a 9-point face, you use one with short- to medium-length ascenders and descenders. It becomes an absolute "must," if you ever simply cannot avoid using an 8-point face. Some art directors feel that longer ascenders and descenders give the copy an elegant appearance, and I can buy into some of that. Also, note how the longer ascenders and descenders force more white space between the lines, giving the copy a more leaded appearance. Sometimes you may want that. Hence, you might occasionally have good reason to use long ascender/descender faces. But always remember that the primary objective is easy readability, and short to medium ascender/descender faces are easiest to read.

About Leading The purpose of leading in regard to easy readability is to permit readers to end one line and, with no effort, find and start the next line. (In addition, leading has an aesthetic function.) Using a typeface with short- to medium-length ascenders and descenders, the old (and easy to remember) rule is that you can set lines about an alphabet-and-a-half (39–40 characters) long without leading and readers will have no difficulty finding the next line.

With lines longer than that, you must start leading because of what the following example says and illustrates:

Copy set too wide is more difficult to read than is copy set to a width which your eyes can read without too much horizontal movement of pupils or head required. Also, especially when copy is set with little or no leading, long lines make it difficult for readers to end a line and then go all the way back across the page to find the next line. I have heard it called "doubling," when people find themselves reading the same line again. Proper leading keeps that from happening.

Attempting to set very narrow lines flush left and right results in some awkward spacing and many hyphenated words.

You can also have a problem with lines set too narrow for flush left and right. Not with leading but with unsightly spacing and too many hyphenated words. To avoid what you see in this example, the solution is: When setting to a very narrow width (e.g., 6 picas), set flush left, *random* right. With copy matter, for good line length and leading, take your cue from newspapers and most magazines: Have lines between 10 and 14 picas wide, with 9- to 12-point type set leaded a point or two.

What about Reverse Type? Primarily, I think, because David Ogilvy gave it so much publicity by saying he would personally strangle with his bare hands any art director using reverse type, I'm always asked this question. It's part of Ogilvy's great showmanship to say such quotable things, but I'm sure he knows there is nothing wrong with reverse type *per se*. (Kids grow up reading reverse type on blackboards.) But to "per se," I add when used in small amounts and correctly, for the problem with reverse type is that it increases the chances of getting bad reproduction.

Printing copy in its normal single color, black, requires one press cylinder to make one impression on the paper. But reverse type is not a color—it's not printing with white ink. It's the paper showing through where the shapes of the letters have been dropped out of the film for the colors. And, when you use reverse with four-color printing, you must have four different cylinders hitting the paper with absolute precision. It's impressive that modern, high-speed presses do it so well so often. But it can and does happen that one or two cylinders will not hit the paper so precisely, and you get "color fill-in"—some of the color dots print inside your lettering, giving you fuzzy, difficult-to-read type.

When you want to use reverse type, ask about a process in which the black film alone makes the outline of the letter, and the other three colors are pulled back a hair from the letter's edge-lines, greatly reducing the possibility of color fill-in. If you look at the letters under a magnifying glass, they will seem to be outlined in black—but naked eyes don't see that. They see only sharp-edged reverse letters. Here are some more tips for using reverse:

- Use it only with a dark, solid-color background, never with a light background. And never use it over a photographic background—if you do that, you'll end up with an unreadable mess.
- Set your type bold, and, if using a serif face, use one with medium contrast between thick and thin strokes, a face in which the "thins" are relatively thick. With a sans serif, never, never use a hairline or light setting.
- Reverse printing can work fine for good, bold headlines (with plain, dark backgrounds). And you can get away with a couple of lines of copy set bold; but don't use reverse for copy blocks longer than, say, four or five lines.

Type as a Graphic   Let's end this chapter on a fun note— but one that is cautionary, too. We can make wonderfully imaginative uses of type and, with specialty faces, add flair to advertisements while, equally important, communicating faster and communicating more than the words themselves "say." But, unless you actually *are* advertising a circus, be careful not to overdo it to the point where your advertisement becomes "circus-y" or where the special effect, instead of working to enhance your message, becomes all that people see and/or remember.

With plain type and imagination, you can, as they did here in an advertisement for stereo equipment, both make readers pause and stop and then dramatize the Propositional Benefit. Also with plain type and imagination and, in this case, with the computer's ability to set print in ways other than in straight and face-on, you can create a curiosity-arousing perspective, and again greatly enhance the Propositional Benefit. What fullness of meaning you get when you come to the word "CRISP"!

If you know that a food menu can include certain specialty choices, you know enough to ask for them. You don't need to know how to prepare them. In the same way, if you know that art directors can do such specialty typographic things as below, you can ask them to experiment when you think it might help you communicate with more dramatic clarity. (Or, if you are an art director, these few examples may encourage you to experiment—remembering the caution that we should use such "tricks" only when it helps communicate, never simply for their own sake.)

Create and photograph the headline For the Mystery Guild book club, an imaginative art director created the classic "clipped-and-pasted-letters" ransom note with the wording of the headline, thereby making not only the words but also the "typography" òf the words add flavor to the meaning of the headline.

With permission of Doubleday Book & Music Clubs, Inc.

Twist it, slant it, do whatever helps Either with the oft-mentioned electronic type setting, or, for small pieces, by hand, we can make the words themselves "act out" their meaning—as *Reader's Digest* did with the article title at left.

And as N.W. Ayer did for a magnificent General Motors booklet-type advertisement on its Total Safety Systems—all the ways it works to make safer cars.

Summary Time

If you are an art director or any other agency person, I hope this chapter either reminded you of the basics of typography or added them to your memory bank. In addition, I hope it gave you a new perspective and opened new vistas to you.

If you are a client, I hope this chapter makes you more of a contributory partner with your agency. I anticipate that when you start to use what you have learned here, some art directors will consider you a pain in the butt. I wouldn't worry about that. Not if you now pay attention to what you never "saw" before. Not if you now ask for typographic skills—and imagination—for which you may never have asked before. Not if you end up with typographically better advertising.

With permission of General Motors Corp.

PART THREE

From Effective
to Great

The Creative Flow Chart and the Two Approaches to Greatness

11

Patterns in Great Advertisements

Until about 15 years ago, whenever I talked or wrote about working in this area, I said (as I have written in this book) that the move from EFFECTIVE to GREAT demands artistry. I said also that there are no rules for artistry, the exercise of that indefinable gift called talent. And I used to leave it at that.

Every time I did, however, I felt unsatisfied with leaving the matter there. I continually wondered: Does that mean there is absolutely *nothing* we can identify and learn about how great advertisements get that way? Must every reach for greatness start from ground zero, and be merely the result of a happy accident? Surely, I reasoned, every great advertisement cannot be *unique* — 100% original, having *nothing* in common with any other great advertisement. There *had* to be some shared qualities, some similar patterns.

Start of a Study Such thinking led me to start collecting and analyzing great print advertisements. Hoping to see any "patterns of greatness." And to learn if they were *continuing* patterns, I decided to include old—even *very* old— advertisements as well as current ones. I selected those that, after many years, remained in everyone's collection of "hall-of-famers." In addition, for them and also for the more recent advertisements, I used a set of criteria that came from three sources: (1) years of contact and conversations on the subject with advertising people who have remained *pragmatic* while succeeding, (2) what *Reader's Digest* had taught me about great print communicating, and (3) my own meshing, molding, and adding to what I learned from those fine teachers.

The Patterns Were There As I studied what I collected, I began to see commonalities first in *mechanics* and then in *qualities*. The more I collected and studied, the more visible and concretely describable they became. Then I found that I could *categorize* groups of advertisements by the *creative tactics* used. The more advertisements I studied and the longer I studied them, the more I found that proved to be definable—thus learnable. I began to call this part of the creative process "method," which, to me, implies a known and workable procedure, broader and less rigid than a rule.

I am now convinced that, in the move from EFFECTIVE to GREAT, we can go *some 90% of the way* with definable, describable, and demonstrable methods. Yes, I know we must still go that last 10%, that surge of...I don't know ...talent, inspiration, genius...that something without which we might reach EXCELLENT but not GREAT. And yes, it seems to me pretentious even to *say* I cannot explain that last 10%. But I have enjoyed rewarding hours with men and women who have exhibited that "something" often enough to make them stars, and *they* never could define it.

I will from here on define, describe, and illustrate what it takes to go 90% of the way. From there, it seems reasonable to believe, you will have a much greater chance of reaching the level of great print advertising than before, because you will know what it takes to get to the threshold; and that level rates as EXCELLENT (way above EFFECTIVE) even if you go no higher.

Creative Flow Chart showing elements of and approaches to Great Print Advertising

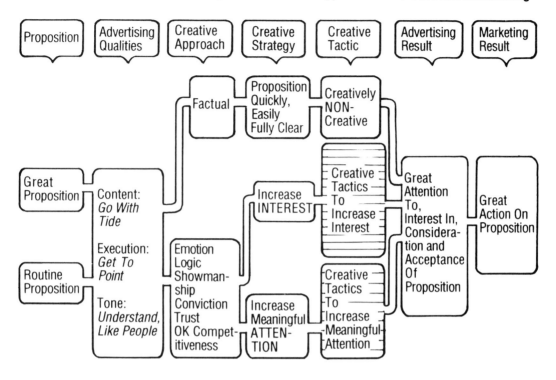

The Creative
Flow Chart

Whenever you must explain something that consists of a number of parts, you obviously cannot blurt out the explanations of all the parts simultaneously. You must take them one by one. Which, in this case, may lead you to think that I will describe a series of *sequential steps*. But I will describe "parts," *not* steps.

I call what you see above a Flow Chart because the "Proposition" *does* always come first, the "Advertising Result" and "Marketing Result" *do* always come last and the advertisement, of course, does come between that beginning and that end. All those boxes between Proposition and Marketing Result relate to parts of the process of creating a great print advertisement. I must explain and illustrate these parts separately. And, when you critique an advertisement, you must analyze each part separately. But, while you and I do our part-by-part work, always keep in mind that we are dealing with a *totality* of parts, not a sequence of steps.

Deliberately Simplified Of course, all advertisement Propositions are not simply "Great" or "Routine." Some are near great, some a little less than that, some a little better than Routine, etc., etc. But to permit us to see and trace the trunk and main branches of the tree, we will ignore all the shoots and leaves of degree and qualification as we work with the Creative Flow Chart to examine how great print advertisements get that way.

What the Boxes Mean What makes a Proposition "great"? That's something like asking, "What makes a taste delicious to everyone?" But I can give a partial and, I believe, useful answer. You can rank a Proposition as "great" *only* when "all those people out there" will immediately *recognize* it as great. How you, personally, rate it doesn't mean a thing. Even if it *is* great, you cannot call if great if "they" cannot immediately understand its significance.

All of which may not come off as very profound. But soon two roads will diverge on the Flow Chart, and which one you take will "make all the difference." And which you take will depend on your evaluation of the Proposition. Thus, the critical ability here will be to make an accurate— a realistic—evaluation. Which you do by calling upon your empathy with people and exercising professional objectivity in that evaluation.

Great Propositions invariably come from the marketing department; rarely are they "created" by the advertising department. For *almost* all advertisements, great or poor, in developing the product and offer, in packaging, in pricing—in all the things marketing does to shape a "package" that will sell—marketing evolves the Proposition. If marketing comes up with a great product or price or whatever, the advertising people get a Great Proposition. (Exception: When a product has no tangible benefit, when any benefit must be *perceived*, its appeal will depend entirely upon the positioning, and that can be done *either* by marketing or by the advertising—and we will go deeper into that in Chapter 12.)

In nearly all cases, it is easy to know when you have been handed a Great Proposition. Simply ask yourself, "If I just plain say it, will that interest, maybe even excite, anybody?" For example, you surely could answer "yes" given the Proposition in the headline at left.

And you could also answer "yes" given this Proposition for Log Cabin maple syrup: **Rich maple taste now has 50%**

Kids stay free at TraveLodge.®

less calories. Or if you had this Proposition: **Introducing The First Disposable Contact Lens**.

Moving on from the Proposition, let's examine the parts that, even though we examine them one by one, remain parts of "the whole." *All* advertisements, great or poor have three parts: **Content, Execution, and Tone**. All *great* advertisements reveal certain *qualities* in each part.

In Content, Go with the Tide "Content" means what the advertisement proposes, literally or by implication. All great advertisements *always* propose what the people at whom they are aimed are ready to accept and are prepared to do or believe. Note "at whom they are aimed." Many different tides run "out there." The trick is to find the potentially most profitable tide for you and go with it. (Just don't try to ride too narrow a tide.)

As with a Great Proposition, being able to go with the tide *almost* always comes from what the marketing department does. If marketing develops a product or offer that goes with the tide, then the advertisement can do so, too. Yes, that does mean—yes, I *do* say—that if marketing develops something nobody wants, no advertising can sell it. At least not without misrepresentation (and then only once).

When the tide is running in the direction of people wanting less fat in their food, McDonald's can run a great advertisement saying **Gimme a big juicy burger with lettuce, tomato, ketchup, mustard, pickles and onions. Hold the fat. New McLean Deluxe. 91% fat-free**. When everyone wants low cholesterol, PAM can run a great advertisement showing a stick of butter with the headline **Get off the stick. (And get off the cholesterol.)** When the tide is running in the direction of people wanting UNscented what they used to want scented, new Unscented Tide goes with the tide (sorry, I couldn't avoid that) when it runs a great advertisement showing a bottle of what it shrewdly French-labeled *Parfum* falling and spilling sickly-yellow contents into clear washing-machine water, capping it with the headline question: **Is there something in your detergent you don't want?** Not too many years ago, these advertisements would not have been written.

In Execution, Get to the Point Advertisements that "creatively hem and haw" before making their Proposition clear get passed by. And advertisements that get passed buy cannot possibly rank as great. Thus, the constant quality of Execution in every great advertisement is that it gets to the point—if not with a single "bam," then with a "bam, bam" or even a "bam, bam, bam." But whether with one shot or two or more rapid-fire shots, they hit hard, fast, and home, like this great advertisement by Bankers Trust (with a bam, bam, bam).

With permission of Bankers Trust Company

An advertisement can "signal" that it will get to the point, but, of necessity, it will take a little time (never too much) to get there. That works, however, *only* if readers immediately understand why it will take longer and will go along with that.

In Tone, Show You Understand and Like People I call it "empathy expressed with a feeling akin to affection," a feeling of "we're on *your* side." I have criticized a headline that said **If you think you know tires, think again.** If you want a great advertisement, it simply cannot be that pugnacious or have a tone that is unpleasant in any way. No more than a salesperson can sass a prospect and expect to sell something.

Great advertisements exhibit such sensitive understanding of people and are so strongly "on their side," that they often make people feel like responding with a *sotto voce* "YEAH!" Anyone who has ever experienced the difference in insurance company attitudes when selling a policy and processing a claim surely muttered "YEAH!" upon seeing this great Independent Insurance Agents advertisement.

When I insured my house, I was Mr. Mayes. When I had a claim, I was Mr. 107-91243.

Not when you deal with an Independent Insurance Agent.

Great or Routine Proposition, Same Qualities We have just covered the three parts of every advertisement, great or poor; I have described the qualities of these parts, which I found in all great advertisements. Those qualities were the same whether the advertisement started with a Great or a Routine Proposition. Thus, on the Flow Chart, both the Great and the Routine Proposition boxes lead into the same box. Now, on the Flow Chart, we move on to the

Approach, Strategy, and Tactic to great advertising when starting with a Great Proposition (APPROACH 1, shaded in gray).

Creative Flow Chart showing elements of and approaches to Great Print Advertising

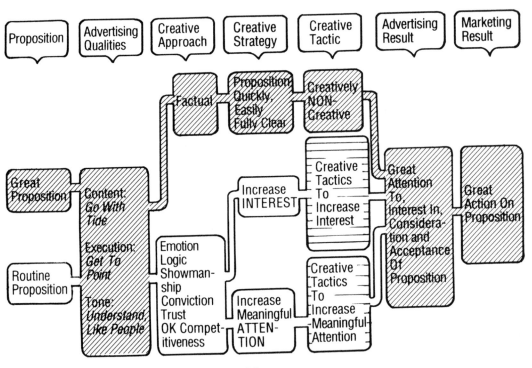

APPROACH 1: Starting with a *Great* Proposition

Starting with a Great Proposition, our **Creative Approach** should be **Factual**. Our **Creative Strategy** should be to **Make the Proposition Quickly, Easily, and Fully Clear**. Our **Creative Tactic** should be **Creatively NON-Creative**—my term for having the creative discipline to not play around when you should not. Almost always, it's best to "just say it." If you can both say it and show it, as Presto does in the great advertisement on the next page, super!

Spray, stream or brush on flavor with Presto® HotTopper™ electric melter/dispenser. A spray of butter for popcorn, a brush of sauce for barbeque, a stream of goodness for your baked potato, warm buttery syrup for pancakes. Melts and warms in minutes. Unplug to use cordless at the table. Immersible for easy cleaning. Even stores toppings in the refrigerator between uses.

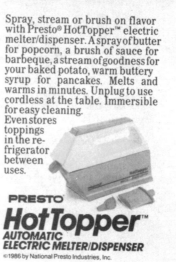

PRESTO
HotTopper™
AUTOMATIC
ELECTRIC MELTER/DISPENSER
©1986 by National Presto Industries, Inc.

With permission of National Presto Industries

Producing a great advertisement when given a Great Proposition should be the easiest thing we do. And, if we follow the right Approach on the Flow Chart, it actually *is* easy to get at least 90% of the way there. The hard part is having the discipline to "stay the course," to resist the temptation to entertain, and to stick to communications. I have written (and truly mean it) that if, while working to communicate, something charming or witty comes to you—something that does not subtract one whit from clarity—go ahead and use it. Wishbone did this with the proposition: "Our new Robusto dressing is even spicier than our regular Italian." They headlined it snappier and more memorably, without losing a bit of clarity. Bravo!

But some may protest, "You can't just say it!" I ask, "Why not?" When I am asked to critique an advertisement with a Great Proposition and do not see the Proposition in the headline, I look immediately at the subhead and the first line of the copy. Almost always, after they have had their fun with a supposedly *keen* headline, they have "just said it" in one of those places. And I am considered "the outside expert" just for telling them, "*There* is your headline.")

Approaches, Strategies, and Tactics when Starting with a Routine Proposition

You may have an old Proposition as good as it ever was, but you've made it so often over so many years it has become Routine. Or maybe it's no longer exclusive, or, like 10% off compared to 50%, it's no scalp-tingler. In short, it's the level of Proposition with which most advertisements must work. Thus, however, it is *also* the level from which most great advertisements start. When we start with a *Routine* Proposition, we still apply the Flow Chart method, but greater artistry in our method is required. And, since artistry does not come easy, we face a considerably more difficult job. But, as just noted, it is the kind of job we must do most often.

We *do* it, however. We produce great print advertisements starting with Routine Propositions—and have done it for generations. Back before most of you were born, all John Caples had to work with was "We propose to teach you by mail to play the piano," a Proposition several other correspondence schools could make and probably were. But with that Routine Proposition, Caples used one of the Creative Tactics we will describe in the next chapter (Walter Mitty) to write his now classic great advertisement **They Laughed When I Sat Down At the Piano—But When I Started to Play!**

For Palmolive Automatic Dishwasher Detergent, they worked with the certainly not exclusive Proposition that the product would, with one washing, clean dishes so thoroughly none would ever have to be returned for another washing. But using another of the Creative Tactics we will describe and illustrate later (Word Play—Clever/Clear), they produced the great advertisement below. (Smartly starting where most people are in these recycling times.)

If there's no stuck-on food or powder residue, there's no re-washing. **Once is all it takes.**

No Deposits. No Returns.

Creative Flow Chart showing elements of and approaches to Great Print Advertising

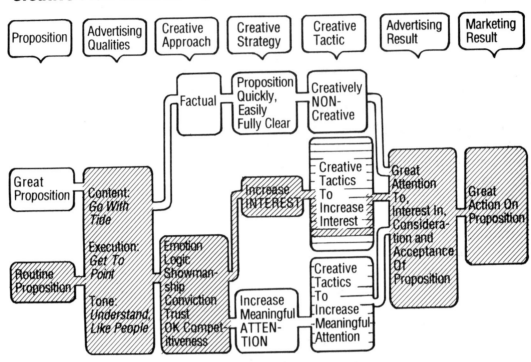

APPROACH 2-A: Starting with a *Routine* Proposition, to Increase INTEREST

Creative Flow Chart showing elements of and approaches to Great Print Advertising

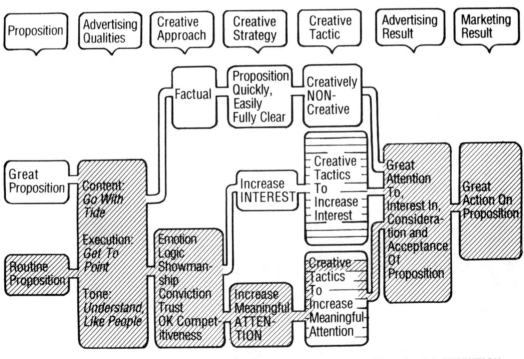

APPROACH 2-B: Starting with a *Routine* Proposition, to Increase Meaningful ATTENTION

Creative Flow Chart showing elements of and approaches to Great Print Advertising

| Proposition | Advertising Qualities | Creative Approach | Creative Strategy | Creative Tactic | Advertising Result | Marketing Result |

APPROACH 2-C: Starting with a *Routine* Proposition, to Increase BOTH

Let's refer again to the Flow Chart to see specifically which Approaches, Strategies, and Tactics we use to try for a great print advertisement when starting with a Routine Proposition. We have three routes we can try. (Obviously, we will use the one that works best.) On this and the previous page (154), I have shaded and numbered them for you on the three reproductions of the Flow Chart (APPROACH 2-A, 2-B, and 2-C). Examine them for a moment; then we will trace each one with descriptions and illustrations.

Starting with a Routine Proposition, we must take the Approach that will have us searching for ways to use—with both skill and artistry—either great **Emotion, Logic, Showmanship, Conviction, Trust,** or what I have termed **OK Competitiveness**.

OK Competitiveness means that you have not competed crudely, brutally, unfairly, or in any way that seems "too much" and possibly embarrasses even the reader. Colgate-Palmolive, a most-often good print advertiser, provides another fine example here: An advertisement showed a humorous photograph of a sheep carrying all its wool from head to mid-body but with its *entire hind-half shorn to the skin* (seeming "naked" from mid-body down). You chuckle the instant you see it then chuckle more when you read the headline **When it comes to hand washables, Palmolive beats the pants off Woolite.** Those chuckles brought by both photograph and headline made this OK Competitiveness. (I'll wager even the Woolite people had to smile.)

What can you do when all you have to propose is that people buy a box of near-universally known (and used) crayons? Well, our kids use crayons to make those drawings over which we parents Oooh and Ah and which we proudly and sentimentally magnet to refrigerator doors. Do you sense Emotion here? The Crayola people surely used Emotion to create this great advertisement:

**The choo-choo that stopped
because Mom forgot the fresh box of Crayola crayons.**

Give them a fresh box and see how they grow.

Increase INTEREST or Meaningful ATTENTION ...or Both? Here's where it becomes a process of back-and-forth, try-and-succeed, or try-and-fail-so-try-something-else. If we could have our druthers, we would prefer to follow the Strategy of trying a Creative Tactic to Increase INTEREST in the Proposition—because that, as I will explain, gets it perceived as more important than it actually is. Or, if none of those Creative Tactics work out for us, we might try the Creative Tactics to Increase Meaningful ATTENTION—because that alone can sometimes produce a great print advertisement. Or, if we really luck out, we might be able to use a combination of Creative Tactics to increase both Meaningful ATTENTION and INTEREST.

Notice I said we would prefer to set our Creative Strategy first (i.e., to Increase INTEREST). But, in my experience, it doesn't work out that way. Instead, you find yourself thinking about which Creative Tactic might work, trying some of them, and when one or a combination does work, that sets your Strategy. It seems backward, I know, but that's how it goes. Provided, of course, that you *know* about the different Creative Tactics that you can try to use. As you will from this book. I will name, describe, and illustrate 25 of them in the next chapter. But first let's finish what we have started by explaining and exemplifying the difference between Increase INTEREST and Increase Meaningful ATTENTION or doing both.

Increasing INTEREST John Caples' "They laughed when I sat down at the piano...." advertisement offers an early—and excellent—example of how to Increase IN-TEREST in a Proposition. You do it by *repositioning* the Proposition so that people *perceive* an offer more substantial, more compelling, and more appealing than the one they would see in the raw proposition. At a party, have you ever sat at a piano, one-fingered chopsticks, and had someone ask, "Do you play?" To which you had to smile sheepishly and say, "Nooooo." But suppose you could have rippled your fingers up and down the keyboard and moved beautifully into some lovely melody, and the other person had turned and called out, "Hey! Come here everybody. Listen to this!" *Wow!* Well, that's what people perceived Caples' famous advertisement to offer. Caples took the Routine Proposition "We propose to teach you by mail to play the piano," and repositioned it to communicate "We propose to make you the life of the party!"

Just once, you should
walk down the same street your
great-grandfather walked.

An airline ran this advertisement proposing that people
fly to Europe—certainly a Routine Proposition. But with
this picture and those words, they repositioned the Proposition to mean much more than a trip to Europe. They made
it a pilgrimage, search for heritage. They touched the same
chord that Alex Haley played so powerfully with *Roots*.

Increasing Meaningful ATTENTION I cry and decry
it every time I hear a big-name advertising person urge
audiences to do advertisements that "get *attention*." Following that superficial urging alone will leave you far short
of the mark you must reach for great advertising. But many
mediocre people do so. Because, throughout their careers,
they remain ignorant of the critical difference between "attention" and "interest"; because it's so easy to get attention
and nothing else; and because their bosses, who also don't
know any better, reward them richly for their "attention-
getting" advertisements.

That's why we see so many advertisements that catch our
eyes but *not our minds*. And that's why, when we start with
a Routine Proposition and cannot get a great print advertisement with the Increase INTEREST strategy and must
go the "attention" route, we must get *Meaningful* ATTEN-
TION. What's the difference? "Hey" gets you meaningless

attention, but "Help" gets you meaningful attention. Because "hey" has no communicating content, and "help" does. Which leads to the point of this section: In reaching for great print advertising, your "call for increased attention" *must* have communicating content, and the content it communicates *must relate to your Propositional Benefit*.

I cannot imagine anyone reading this book who would not know the Timex watch Proposition of excellent watches at relatively low prices. Having long ago set the "price half" of the Proposition in people's minds (and with shoppers seeing such good prices every time they come across the watches on display), Timex now puts its advertising emphasis on reminding people of its styling, accuracy, durability—on the fact that Timex does indeed make excellent watches.

TIMEX WATCHES.
TOO GOOD TO KEEP UP YOUR SLEEVE.

From me, this great British Timex advertisement got extra attention, and *Meaningful* ATTENTION because it fast-replayed in my mind still another repeating of the Timex Proposition I know by heart. Look at the Creative Flow Chart. Note that you follow a particular Creative *Strategy* by executing a particular Creative *Tactic*. This great advertisement uses a Tactic I call "Vivid Visualization."

Increasing Both INTEREST and Meaningful ATTENTION Sometimes it's possible to increase both INTEREST and Meaningful ATTENTION by using a combination of two Creative Tactics for the same advertisement—

one that works to Increase INTEREST in the Proposition by repositioning it, and another that attracts Increased Meaningful ATTENTION to the advertisement.

The 18 week Charles Atlas course as paid for by H. M. Government.

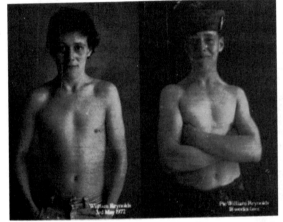

For all we know, you could be a born leader.

A genius at tactics.

You may be able to shoot ants' eyebrows off at 500 metres.

But if you're unfit, you're not much use to the Army.

And that's why the major part of the 18 weeks you'll spend in Basic Training is devoted to getting you fit.

By 'fit', we don't mean being able to run up a few flights of stairs without passing out.

We're talking about being hard enough to run for 10 miles in full battle kit carrying a 9lb rifle.

"You must be joking" we can hear you muttering.

"I wouldn't last a week."

You're wrong. And we can prove it.

To start with, we put you through a tough medical to make sure you're up to it.

Then, when the training gets under way, we check you again to find out just how fit you are.

The results tell us how hard we can push you.

In charge of all this is your P.T. Instructor.

He's trained to spot when a bloke's had enough, and when he can do with a bit more. Like 2 miles round the barracks and an extra 50 press-ups.

For the first month or so, you might want to put arsenic in his tea.

But as the weeks pass, your beer gut will start to disappear.

Your lungs will start coping with a 4 mile run without bursting into flames.

Your arms, chest and legs will begin shaping up into something you're not ashamed to look at.

At which point you might well thank the bloke for getting you fitter and stronger than you've ever been in your life.

And that's not just a bonus for you. It's good for us. Because the British Army is not accustomed to having sand kicked in its face.

If you've got it in you, we'll bring it out.

To: Army Careers, P.O. Box 1EL, London W1A 1EL. I'd like to know more about soldiering. Please send me more information about The Professionals.

Name _____

Address _____

_____

Tel: _____ Age ____ yrs ____ mths.

The Professionals 🇬🇧

This great British Army recruiting advertisement uses a combination of the Creative Tactics I call "Walter Mitty" and "Oh, I get it." The "Walter Mitty" tactic gets Increased INTEREST by repositioning the raw Proposition of "join the Army" to "in just 18 weeks, change yourself from a scrawny, timid kid to a confident, muscular man"—the same compelling appeal of the original Charles Atlas "I'll make you a man" advertisements. Simultaneously, the "Oh, I get it" tactic works by presenting a little something for you to figure out in the headline and illustrations. You can't resist doing it, and as you "get it," you give the advertisement Increases Meaningful ATTENTION.

Do you see where we are on the Flow Chart? In the middle, where we follow a Creative Strategy by executing one of its Creative Tactics or a combination of Strategies by executing two appropriate Tactics. In the next chapter, I will describe and illustrate the 25 repeatedly used Creative Tactics that I have, thus far, been able to identify by collecting and studying great print advertisements.

25 Creative Tactics for Great Print Advertisements Starting with Routine Propositions

12

To review very briefly where we are on the Creative Flow Chart: What we will cover now all comes under the heading of "Creative Tactic": the 25 Creative Tactics that I have thus far been able to confirm as *known* Creative Tactics by finding them in enough advertisements over a long enough period of time. Some 15 Increase INTEREST in a Routine Proposition by, in effect, *repositioning* it to get it perceived as somehow more substantial, more fundamental, or more important than the actual Proposition. Another 10 Increase Meaningful ATTENTION. "Meaningful" because it communicates the Proposition and gets still another registration of it.

Known Creative Tactics to Increase INTEREST

1. Justified Pride With this Creative Tactic, you can add significant weight to your Routine Proposition by exhibiting responsible or assertive—or sometimes even humorous or cocky—pride in your product. But the Tactic carries a big "IF." You can use it only IF most people will accept your pride as *justified*.

Back in 1914, Americans certainly granted Cadillac Motor Car Company its claim as "The Standard of the World," and they received as fully justified Cadillac's now classic advertisement **The PENALTY OF LEAD-ERSHIP**. (When you are the leader you are everyone's target and you must work constantly to stay ahead of competition.) As an American, I cheer Cadillac's 1990s comeback and regret having to write that, only few years ago, many Americans would not have accepted such pride as justified. But today they certainly would (and did) accept as justified the pride that Whirlpool exhibited with this headline and copy, which surely got more interest than the typical appliance advertisement and worked to make buying anything with the Whirlpool name more significant:

We all know what happened to America's quality standards, which no doubt explains why we have seen only a few current advertisements using this tactic. But if you believe, as I do, that Americans have now become sufficiently aroused to earn back our reputation for high quality, look for more great print advertisements using this Tactic.

2. You Can Do It . . . Easily This goes way back and remains a known Creative Tactic for great print advertising of products that offer people opportunities to do what they want to (or must) do, but want to do *in the easiest way*. When Kodak introduced its Brownie camera, many people were eager to take the new "snapshots," but they apparently hesitated because it seemed so complicated or technical. Kodak reassured them and opened the Snapshot Age with one of the earliest great print advertisements using this Tactic: ***"You press the button, we do the rest."***

I can't think of any household chores that better fit the description of "must be done but want an easy way" than washing clothes or dishes. No surprise, then, that laundry soaps used this tactic from the beginning.

Who else wants a *whiter* wash
– with no hard work ?

HOW would you like to see your wash come out of a simple soaking—whiter than hours of scrubbing could make it!

Millions of women do it every week. They've given up washboards for good. They've freed themselves *forever* from the hard work and reddened hands of washday.

Now they just soak—rinse—and hang out to dry! In half the time, without a bit of hard rubbing, the wash is on the line—*whiter than ever!*

Dirt floats off—stains go

The secret is simply Rinso—a mild, granulated soap that gives rich, lasting suds even in the hardest water.

Just soak the clothes in the creamy Rinso suds—and the dirt and stains float off. Rinse—and the wash is spotless.

Even the most soiled parts need only a gentle rub between the fingers to make them snowy. Thus clothes last longer, for there's no hard rubbing against a board.

Safe for clothes, easy on hands

No laundry soap is easier on clothes or on hands than Rinso. Contains no acids, harsh chemicals or bleaches—nothing to injure white clothes or fast colors.

Rinso is all you need on washday. No bar soaps, chips or powders. Get Rinso for small cost from your grocer. Follow easy directions on package.

Use in washing machines

Rinso is wonderful in washers. Recommended by 23 leading washing machine makers for safety, and for a whiter, cleaner wash.

"Rinso suds soak everything clean, so I have no more boiling to do, no hard rubbing on a washboard. Little wonder that my clothes last a lot longer. And Rinso isn't hard on my hands, either. I have used all kinds of laundry soaps—bar soaps and chip soaps—for a good many years, but nothing but Rinso for me, now. It makes my washday so easy and my clothes so white and bright. Rinso deserves to be the Boston woman's very own laundry soap."

MRS. GEO. N. TAPP
13 Haviland St.
Boston, Mass.

Millions use Rinso. Thousands write us letters like this.

Mrs. G. N. Tapp, a Hub woman, says:

As this great Rinso advertisement illustrates. (Incidentally, note the astute words "Who else . . ." with its prodding implication that many others now enjoy this benefit, "why not you?")

Electrasol,® another consistently excellent print advertiser, provides an example that *today's* detergents still use
this Creative Tactic to go from Routine (i.e., nonexclu-
sive) Propositions to great print advertisements. This one
seems so simple in headline and photograph and is so
great *precisely for that reason.* I cannot imagine any reader
glancing—even idly—at the head and art and not getting
still another—and *very strong*—registration of Electrasol's
well-known Proposition.

3. Repeated Great Line When using this Tactic, you
develop for or about your product a great line that you
repeat and repeat until it takes on the ring of capital
"T" Truth. Obviously, this takes *many* advertisements—
sometimes *years*—to pay off. But once it starts to, you
have something that can actually go into the company
books as a valuable asset. Although one of the oldest Creative Tactics, it comes into today as powerful and as frequently used as ever: **Good Morning, have you used Pears
Soap?** (1890s); **Hasn't scratched yet. So use Bon Ami.**
(1930s); **Aren't you glad you use Dial? Don't you wish**

everyone did? (1960s); **Reach out, reach out and touch someone.** (1970-80s); and so on. Many such lines seem to have been gospel as long as we can remember: **A diamond is forever; When you care enough to send the very best; Let your fingers do the walking; Good to the last drop; Fly the friendly skies..;** and one I was so happy to see my good friends at Campbell Soup bring back: **Mm! Mm! Good!** Any of us could keep adding and adding to the list of Repeated Great Lines. And, to me, slogans like these go beyond underpinning great advertisements. Perhaps because they express the longevity of good things, they comfort me. Each time I read one, it adds to my sense of "all's right with the world."

4. Short Short Story Readers love little stories and anecdotes. If you can put your Routine Proposition into one of these forms, you can write an advertisement that people *cannot stop reading* once they start. And, possibly, you can get your Routine Proposition perceived as at least *near-profound* if not actually so.

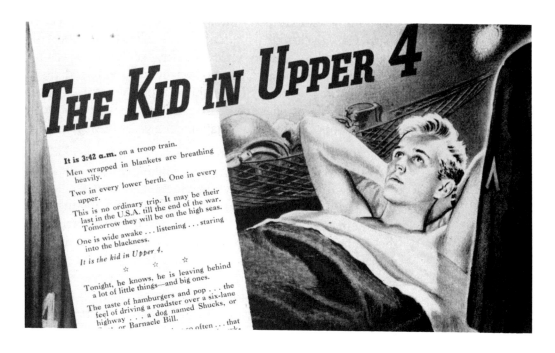

The classic in this category is, I believe, the New Haven Railroad advertisement above proposing that passengers not get angry if, during World War II, they couldn't get a seat on a train, or a berth, or had to wait to get into the dining car. The copy began, "**It's 3:42 a.m. on a troop train.** [Once you started, could you stop reading?] **Men wrapped in blankets are breathing heavily. Two in every lower berth. One in every upper. This is no ordinary trip. It may be their last in the U.S.A. till the end of the war. Tomorrow they will be on the high seas. One is wide awake . . . listening . . . staring into the blackness. *It is the kid in Upper 4.*"**

Another advertisement by IBM carried no headline. It "opened" with a close-up photograph of the midriff of a man in a business suit, one arm forward, and extending out of the shirt cuff was not a normal hand but a steel prosthesis holding an IBM calling card. Directly beneath, in good-size type, the copy begins: "**The man behind this hand is Michael Coleman. The company behind this man is IBM. There's a story behind both of them. After the Marines and Vietnam, . . .** " There is *no way* you could stop reading about what so many equally fine companies could write about: The not surprising achievements of disabled employees. A great print advertisement, using the Creative Tactic of Short Short Story.

I cannot end this section without mentioning Maytag's many, *many* years of using story-type advertisements with black-and-white family-style pictures of couples telling about their long use of Maytag washers, driers, and dishwashers. With these Short Short Story advertisements, Maytag has gotten repeated readings of its very well-known proposition to buy Maytags for years of dependable service.

5. Walter Mitty   These days, very few remember—or have even *heard* of—Danny Kaye playing the role of the timid Walter Mitty, who daydreamed of himself as a swashbuckling hero. However, whether or not anyone remembers the name, the Creative Tactic, so solidly rooted in human psychology, remains fertile. You employ it by getting your Routine Proposition perceived as a promise to make people somehow more important, more daring, or more romantic— more whatever it is that people might *yearn to be* instead of just plain themselves.

Do you remember seeing a reproduction of David Ogilvy's famous Hathaway Shirt advertisement showing a distinguished gentleman wearing an *eye-patch?* The raw proposition rated no better than that which any other good shirt company could make. But that man with the eye-patch made the advertisement say, "This distinguished, obviously cultured gentleman also is a *real* man, with adventure in his background—maybe a war or a duel or maybe a fancy lady scratched his eye. Now, all you Walter Mittys, shouldn't you wear the same linen as he does?"

Ogilvy has said that he used the eye-patch to give the advertisement "story value"—I believe along the lines I have just described. But many advertising people have completely misunderstood that classic advertisement, thinking of the eye-patch as only a gimmick, and that the gimmick in itself was everything. Even the Hathaway people seemed not to understand it when, not long ago, they ran an advertisement showing two football coaches wearing eye-patches. If you agree with them and consider the eye-patch only an attention-getting gimmick, consider this: Suppose Ogilvy had used an even *stronger* attention-getting gimmick—a bone through the gentleman's nose. Seeing this, do you suppose anyone would want to buy and wear the same shirt as that man?

With permission of Clyde Bartel

Today, we could fit the Marlboro cowboy into the Walter Mitty category. And when Barney's put its now-routine proposition of extensive selection of famous-label men's clothing in an advertisement headline **How the men who run things identify one another,** they used the Walter Mitty tactic, too.

I regret not seeing this Tactic used much any more because it leaves little used a still-strong Tactic for great advertising. Its neglect stems, I believe, from what has happened to many of us who *make* advertising—not anything that has happened to those who *read* it. Many "makers" have turned self-consciously "sophisticated" and uncomfortable with this seemingly corny Tactic. But, friends, all those people out there still have their fantasies. They still yearn to be "more" in so many ways. Offer to help them, and they will come to you.

6. Proposition Challenge You execute this Tactic by presenting the proposition in the form of an easily understood and (critically important) *easy-to-accept* challenge. The earliest use of the Tactic I found turned a Routine Proposition to improve your grammar into the hall-of-fame **Do You Make These Mistakes in English?** A modern use of it turned the Routine Proposition of "Be a male nurse" into the challenging and great British advertisement you see here.

Are you man enough to do women's work?

The work is nursing, and the answer is it's probably too tough for most people.

Because nurses are expected to respond confidently and efficiently to any emergency from fractures to heart attacks.

Squeamish about injections? An 18-year-old nurse has to give them.

Acquire the knack of working with others in skilled teams.

While remaining cheerful and optimistic even when the odds seem stacked against them.

Precious few people can claim that ability. Male *or* female.

As a nurse, you'll have a career to think about too, not just a job.

You could become a Charge Nurse managing your own ward and its nurses.

If you're career minded, a Nursing Officer responsible for three or more wards, a unit of operating theatres or a coronary or renal unit.

And if you're really ambitious it won't end there.

Now, obviously, you'll need a thorough training for a job where people's lives are at stake.

Do you know a Mosquito Forceps from a Spencer Wells?

But no time is wasted in getting you on the wards.

Before long, you'll find yourself observing major operations.

And, later on, helping in an intensive care team.

If that sounds hard it's because it is.

But if you qualify

It's easy. He'd be a trouble breathing. I could you help?

A Defibrillator: you'll have to learn how to use one.

nursing offers as challenging and worthwhile a career as you'll find.

So if you've always looked on nursing as strictly women only, remember the sex discrimination laws work both ways.

In fact, there's nothing to stop you entering any branch of nursing you like.

If you're man enough, that is.

For more information, post this coupon to The Chief Nursing Officer, Dept of Health and Social Security (BTVi), PO Box 702, London SW20 8SZ.

Name _____ Age _____

Address _____

Nursing.

It's not just your own life you make the best of.

If I were an agency creative director, a dental floss would sit high on my list of accounts I would *not* relish having—*what* is there to *say?* But then I would have been shamed by an advertisement for Johnson's Dental Floss made great through the Proposition Challenge Tactic: It showed a nice set of teeth inside a partially opened, attractive mouth under the headline **If you fail**

this simple test you could lose your teeth. Then, call-out lines (running from teeth and gums to captions) asked me four questions I could not resist answering. In the process of answering those questions, Johnson's Dental Floss became much more interesting to me than before.

7. Go Beyond Product Features A long-used Creative Tactic to Increase INTEREST in a by-now Routine Proposition. And also another that must be used over a long period of time to really pay off. An advertisement using this tactic doesn't sell what the product *is,* and it doesn't sell product *physical features* that the competition can match. The advertisement sells what the product *does* for you, for your life, and tries to claim and preempt a unique benefit or to portray the benefit in a way that makes any similar portrayal seem like mere imitation.

I said *"long-used."* In 1914, when Pyrene advertised its fire extinguisher, they went beyond the brass and nickel-plated casing, beyond the easy pump-action. They did not propose people buy the extinguisher for its physical or mechanical features. They proposed that people buy *peace of mind*, safety for their families. That was before my time, but I assume the competition could have, and soon *did*, copy the product features. But once Pyrene said *"...and Pyrene Saved Us,"* no one could copy that.

I said *"must be used over a long period."* For years now, Johnson & Johnson has *not* tried to sell the physical properties of its baby products. It has—with magnificent success—proposed that by using them, you express a mother's love. Johnson & Johnson has, with many great advertisements using this Tactic, preempted that benefit.

Ethan Allen Galleries did some great print advertisements using this Tactic. One of the series showed a lovely photograph of a mother reading to a child in bed. The headline said **The bedtime story is more important than the bed**. That advertisement moved beyond product features—beyond good colonial furniture—which, of course, other companies can and do make, too. If continued, such advertising could earn for Ethan Allen a valuable image no other company could then copy: Their furniture is part of a good home and a loving family life.

8. Personify This must have been one of Leo Burnett's favorite Creative Tactics for great print advertising. From his agency have come the Marlboro cowboy, the Jolly Green Giant, and Tony the Tiger, among others. This Tactic, like Repeated Great Line and Go Beyond Product Features, requires repeated use and has a long history. Even a wonderfully tenacious librarian at Campbell Soup could not pinpoint the *exact* birth year of **The Campbell Kids**. Most likely, those cheerful, rosy-cheeked kids started helping to make Campbell Soup advertisements great in about 1900. And the last time I talked with my friends in Camden, NJ, they planned to bring the Kids back along with **Mm! Mm! Good!**

Today, how do you make great advertisements that put into millions of American minds unforgettable pictures that get people to buckle their seat belts? Create two lovable dummies (called Vince and Larry), and, with a touch of humor, have them do and talk about all sorts of dangerous (and dumb) things—things that would make any of us feel sheepishly guilty—and vow never to do them again. And who Personified this so often repeated (and ignored) message to make it now so memorably demanding? Leo Burnett, bless 'em! (See next page.)

With permission of U.S. Dept. of Transportation via Leo Burnett USA

Certainly, through the years, a straw-hatted, aproned, celluloid-collared New Englander named **Titus Moody** has added substantially to each Pepperidge Farm proposition to buy its bakery products. Likewise, Jack Daniel Distillery has used the **friendly distillery workers of Lynchburg, Tennessee**, for many, many years to greatly increase interest in what might have been just another claim of bourbon smoothness. (In fact, Jack Daniel's black-and-white-picture-and-large-copy advertisements lay claim to being the "longest-running-same-format" advertisements in history—38 years as of 1992!)

9. "Quiet" Statement This Creative Tactic to Increase INTEREST in routine propositions and produce great print advertisements uses a "quiet, reasonable voice" in the babble of advertising "shouting." It is completely in accord with human nature for such a voice to receive greater respect and authority than does that of the shouter.

In a carnival of weight-reducing product advertising, Mead Johnson introduced Metrecal as an OTC product this way: Under a simple headline saying **A public statement concerning Metrecal, a new concept in weight control**, they ran four columns of type—no pictures, no hype. They even got the advertisement reviewed and approved by the Department of Advertising Evaluation of the American Medical Association—and said so in a note with the advertisement. This "Quiet" Statement great advertisement contributed to an extraordinarily successful product introduction.

As part of the introduction of Dove bar, Lever Brothers ran a similarly "quiet" advertisement—all type except for small blue drawings under the headline **SUDDENLY, Soap Is Old-Fashioned.** It carried a coupon, and this one long-copy, calmly explanatory advertisement sold *2,800,000* bars of Dove, prompting Lever to call it the single most successful advertisement in its history to that time!

I play golf with a man who truly deserves the title of "gentleman." He demonstrated it in business, too, when, as President of the American Tobacco Company, he himself wrote what has to be the most quiet advertisement ever run by any cigarette company. Except for the Surgeon General's warning required, you are looking at the entirety of this extraordinary and, I believe, great print advertisement.

If you smoke
please try Carlton.

With permission of The American Tobacco Company

10. Testimonial Another long, extensively, and still used Creative Tactic to Increase INTEREST in Routine Propositions, but it is one that, for *great* print advertisements, has changed. The bulk of run-of-the-mill testimonial advertising still features famous personalities endorsing products. And that's OK when the personalities clearly have the credentials to judge what they endorse, and/or have solid credibility with the public for some reason. (Witness long-time knee pain sufferer Joe Namath's powerful job for Chattem's Flex-all 454®.) But some years ago we saw so many obviously paid and unqualified "witnesses," that the Tactic lost its value—so much so that the Skippy peanut butter people did a great print advertisement by *making fun of it*. They showed Casey Stengel saying, in essence, "Sure they paid me to say I like Skippy . . . but I *do* and would have said it for nothing."

But past and current misuse does not keep the Testimonial Tactic from being used—*astutely*—to produce great print advertisements. "Astutely" today appears to mean using actual consumers more than famous people, and that the consumers must offer either very logical reasons for their satisfaction or factual benefits they have enjoyed. Tylenol offers an excellent example: A smiling middle-aged woman—attractive but obviously not a model and with her name and town given—"looks" directly at you, the reader. The headline, with quotation marks signifying her speaking, reads **"I stopped using aspirin the day the hospital gave me Tylenol®."** What a logical and believable reason to switch, and given by a real person who seems to have no selfish reason for doing so. Another example, shown elsewhere in this book, is the Dove advertisement that contains signatures of real women testifying to what Dove did for their skin in seven days.

Bayer demonstrated another version of the Testimonial Tactic—third party (but not personal) endorsement of a Proposition. When news first broke about research showing that an aspirin a day helps reduce incidence of heart attack and stroke, a great Bayer advertisement showed several newspaper clippings headlining the news. Over the clippings appeared the headline **News that could help save your life is making news**.

11. It's OK to Do Suppose you have to make a Routine Proposition that people do something they *want* to do but hesitate because it may be unhealthy (e.g., smoking) or because they think they would be embarrassed to do it. The Creative Tactic that has, under such conditions, produced great print advertisements gives people *an acceptable rationale for doing it*.

Clairol faced the "embarrassment" obstacle in the early days of hair coloring. Many women very much *wanted* to do it. But, back then, many still called it "dyeing" or "bleaching," and it still carried the stigma of being something ladies of quality did not do. Enter a remarkable campaign of great print advertisements carrying the headline **Does she … or doesn't she?** Enter also another case of many advertising professionals misunderstanding advertisements. The campaign certainly helped bring in a time when millions of women color their hair without embarrassment. But many in advertising believe it did so *only* because of the promise that women could do it without anyone else knowing.

The copy of these advertisements *did* say the product, Miss Clairol, would color hair naturally—"so natural only her hairdresser knows for sure." But is that *all* the advertisements "said" to women? No, they said *much* more, and perhaps more with the *artwork* than with the copy. The copy mentioned "... the kind of woman who always finds time for a quiet half-hour *with her child*" (my italics). The photography set that image even more strongly, each one showing a *lovely mother* with a *sweet young child*. That artwork got the proposition perceived not only as color your hair naturally but also, and *more* so, as color your hair the way these *quality ladies*—these *mothers*—do.

For years, in seminars, I have shown the Clairol advertisement on the screen, leaving the copy saying "Colors your hair naturally." But, over the pictures of the wholesome ladies and mothers, I superimpose a picture like the one here. Then I ask, "The copy still says colors your hair naturally. But with art like that would those advertisements have assured millions of women that it was OK to do?" The laughter has provided the answer.

Now that cigarette advertising must put Surgeon General's warnings in every advertisement, "It's OK to do" is the only Creative Tactic that can produce great advertising there. But fortunately (says this ex-heavy smoker who admits there is nothing worse than a reformed sinner), the cigarette people seem not to have done much with it. With *one exception:* Virginia Slims' **You've come a**

long way, baby *does* reposition the Routine Proposition perfectly to have it perceived as "be a liberated woman"— and that proposition certainly does go with the female tide.

12. That Makes Sense This seems to have been a favorite Creative Tactic of the old Doyle Dane Bernbach, during the days of its great advertisements for Volkswagen, Avis, and Levy's bread. When all the great Beetle advertisements said, in essence, **this car is so homely because it's so mechanically perfect**, people who were suffering mechanical *im*perfection with the big tail-fin cars of that time responded, "That makes sense." When the Avis advertisements said, **"When you're No. 2, you must try harder,"** people again felt, "That makes sense." When a Levy's advertisement showed a little African-American boy enjoying a slice of rye bread under the headline **You don't have to be Jewish to love Levy's bread,** people chuckled, "That makes sense."

Back in the 1930s, when Ford and Chevrolet had the low-priced car field to themselves, Plymouth wanted to break into that market. But, since the public wasn't clamoring for that to happen, Plymouth had only a Routine Proposition to make. At that time, however, Chrysler had a president almost as famous and forceful as Lee Iacocca. And after they created and ran these great advertisements, with Walter P. Chrysler suggesting something that got millions of people to think, "That makes sense," the American language got a new phrase: "The low-priced *three*."

"Look at All Three!

BUT DON'T BUY ANY LOW-PRICED CAR UNTIL YOU'VE DRIVEN THE NEW PLYMOUTH WITH FLOATING POWER"

Turning the pages of a business magazine, readers came upon a page with these words in large type: **Would you tolerate an employee who's anti-social, temperamental, abuses power, wastes office supplies, antagonizes other employees, requires constant professional help and makes a habit of taking unscheduled vacations?** When readers turned the page, they saw the headline **Then fire your copier.** I'm sure that made sense to executives whose copiers gave them such grief. From a routine proposition that all copiers make ("we're dependable"), Ricoh got a great print advertisement using the That Makes Sense Tactic.

13. Yes, *That's* True   This is close to "That Makes Sense," but a distinctly *different* Creative Tactic. As with all Tactics for producing great advertising, this one goes along with human nature, specifically the way we respond enthusiastically to statements with which we agree. "Give your children Kool-Aid" is by now a Routine Proposition; but **You loved it as a kid. You trust it as a mother.** makes people smile, "Yes, *that's* true." A simple drink thus becomes a fondly perceived part of our lives. And Kraft General Foods makes still another great print advertisement (they make so *many*) starting with a Routine Proposition.

Suppose you were a salesman and the man at left was your prospect. And when you first called on him he said, **"I don't know who you are. I don't know your company. I don't know your company's product. I don't know what your company stands for. I don't know your company's customers. I don't know your company's record. I don't know your company's reputation. Now—what was it you want to sell me?"** All that appeared in a hall-of-fame advertisement with a routine proposition: Advertise in a business publication. But when McGraw-Hill Magazines ran that great advertisement, which included **MORAL: Sales start before your salesman calls...**, sales people everywhere sighed, "Yes...oh yes, that's true."

14. *Profitable* Public Service   To execute this Creative Tactic, you make advertisements that, to some or total extent, perform a public or personal service. Readers give it Increased INTEREST because of that, and perceive the Routine Proposition as having significantly more than ordinary weight. But note that word "profitable." While performing a bona fide public service, the advertisement logically and deservedly sells the product. The "old" classic in this category: Caterpillar's advertisement showing a soot-covered, dead-tired man in a hard hat, leaning on a tractor blade, with the headline **Ever watch a forest die?** The copy made an eloquent plea for more careful use of our forest lands, and included, logically and deservedly, how Caterpillar equipment works to protect them.

Shell Oil Company provides the best contemporary example of this Tactic. Surely, you have seen those bright yellow booklet-type advertisements that provide a wealth of expert and useful information about driving and taking care of your car and home. They first came out some years ago, and ran through a series of over 30! I have been told that, when the series started, some of the more "practical-minded" in the company asked, in essence, "Why are we fooling around with that stuff? We should be selling Shell gasoline." Well, during the first several-year run of these advertisements, Shell gasoline sales went from No. 3 to No. 1! I call that *Profitable* Public Service. At this writing, the booklet advertisements are running again, as great as before.

The people who make and sell Bac★Os® demonstrated that you can use this Creative Tactic for lighter subjects, too. Whether you should chop or tear lettuce may not be a momentous question, but people (including me) have wondered about it a long time, and they (and I) found Increased INTEREST in an advertisement under the heading **SALAD TIPS 'N BITS No. 2 CHOPPING VS. TEARING,** which provided the service of an answer. *Profitable* Public Service.

15. Heaven Forbid! In this case, the Routine Proposition relates to something people don't want to happen to them; and the Creative Tactic is to magnify—even over-dramatize—what people want to avoid. And we have here another still-potent Creative Tactic that many of us seem to have become too "sophisticated" to use. We see it only rarely now. Perhaps we cannot use it as melodramatically as we once did, but we still can—and do, as I note below—use the Tactic to go from Routine Propositions to great print advertisements.

At the time Listerine ran this now-classic great advertisement, there were already enough other products available to make "avoid unpleasant breath" a Routine Proposition, certainly not exclusive. But Listerine, which had already "magnified" the problem by using the word "halitosis," proposed more here than "avoid unpleasant breath." They actually proposed: "Don't drift into a lifetime of heartbroken loneliness." *Heaven Forbid!*

Today, we know it is bad to use too much salt. And a product called NoSalt™ offered an alternative (salt flavor without sodium) with a great advertisement using the Heaven Forbid Tactic. A bold headline asked **Are you a saltaholic?**—evoking images of calling someone at 3 A.M., pleading, "Come help me, I'm about to eat some salt!" And the advertisement's three quick questions, to which most of us would *have* to answer "yes," identified *me* as among "most Americans" who consume 20 times more salt than we need. Am I a saltaholic? *Heaven Forbid!* Yes, this was done with a bit of tongue-in-cheek, but it carried—and with the Tactic got Increased INTEREST in—a serious product message.

Known
Creative Tactics
to Increase Meaningful ATTENTION

Sometimes getting Increased Meaningful ATTENTION tends to increase intensity of interest as well. But we can produce great print advertisements without doing that because (1) we can capitalize on already high interest or (2) our proposition, while now Routine because we have made it so often for so long, remains as good as ever, and what we want are repeated memory-reinforcing registrations of it. I found the following Creative Tactics being used for such situations to produce great print advertisements.

1. Oh, I Get It! The largest number of great print advertisements in my collection use this tactic. The headline and/or major illustration playfully present a little something to figure out. You cannot resist trying, you quickly *"get it"* you feel delighted with your sharpness—and you have given the Increased Meaningful ATTENTION that makes an advertisement great.

THE PFIZER HEALTHCARE SERIES

You can tell
high blood pressure
by these symptoms:

_____

_____

_____

_____

_____

(Very often, there are none!)

Capitalizing on already existing interest, Pfizer ran a great print advertisement with this headline and the blank lines, and you "got it" before the subhead gave what is probably news to you—that often there are *no* symptoms. By far most often, I found this Tactic used to get another and memorable registration of a well-known, good-as-ever proposition:

- You see a woman with a water bucket applying a large sponge to beautiful flower-pattern wallpaper and the headline: **Some of our most attractive flowers can now stand quite a watering.** You get it: wallpaper you can wash.
- You see a smugly smiling middle-aged man and the headline: **"Yesterday, I kept four women happy while I was tied up."** Then you see a telephone answering machine, and you get it. He bought a machine and recorded his messages.
- You see a picture of a dollop of mayonnaise that is obviously *cut in half* and the headline: **Until now, if you wanted all the taste of regular mayonnaise with only half the calories, you had to sacrifice something.** You don't even have to see (but you do) the jar of Kraft Light Reduced Calorie Mayonnaise to get it: You had to sacrifice half of what you wanted.
- Under a headline asking, **Heard any good pickles lately?** you see a firm pickle just that instant snapped in half and surrounded by flying droplets of water. You get it: pickles so crunchy fresh they audibly snap when you break them.

I could go on and on, but I can give each Tactic only so much space. I hope these were enough illustrations to help you *get* this Tactic.

2. Ink/Paper Special Effects   Essentially, you execute this Tactic successfully by thinking not only of "saying" and "showing" but also of *"dramatizing"*—and dramatizing in some special, unexpected way. You use it the same way you sometimes use camera special effects. Disney, THE master of special effects in motion pictures, proved itself a master in print as well with what I consider one of the best Ink/Paper Special Effects I've ever seen. On the next page, look at the newspaper special effect advertising one of its films and using this Tactic to Increase Meaningful Attention—as powerfully and irresistably as the natural force it dramatizes.

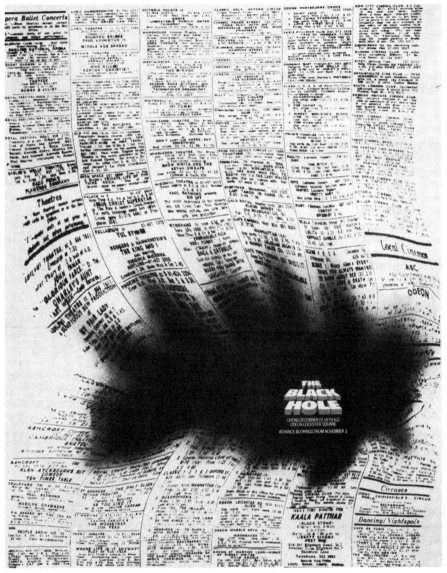

Another advertisement I will never forget used this Tactic for Lucite paint. When you came to *that* newspaper page, it looked like someone had dripped paint all over it. The Proposition? Use Lucite paint because it won't drip "like this" while you're painting. The Special Effect got truly Meaningful Increased ATTENTION! An Ink/Paper Special Effect does not have to be as extraordinary as those two examples. It can be as simple as a headline that was

*A letter
to an an old friend
shouldn't look like*
`a letter to
your attorney.`

intended to get Increased Meaningful ATTENTION for a Proposition to buy a typewriter that offers easily changeable typefaces. (At left.)

3. GOTCHA! Another very frequently used Creative Tactic to get great print advertisements out of Routine Propositions. The advertisement lures people "in" then charmingly, humorously—*never* offensively—it blindsides them with the point! The "ancestor" that I found—and which ran back when people had their jewelry copied and kept the real stuff in the safe—carried the headline **A $10,000 Mistake.** The copy read, **"A client for whom we had copied a necklace of Oriental Pearls, seeing both necklaces before her, said: "Well the resemblance is remarkable, but this is mine!"** [New paragraph] **Then she picked up ours!"** GOTCHA!

Chivas Regal (which has done so *many* great print advertisements) pictured an empty Chivas bottle. The first line of a two-line headline said: **Chivas Regal is always twelve years old.** The second line said: **Rarely thirteen.** GOTCHA!

When you come upon this great advertisement for the Purina Pets For People Program™ and see the first picture of the unhappy gray-haired man, you cannot stop your eyes following the sequence right to the headline. GOTCHA!

With permission of Ralston-Purina Co. and Judson Morgan

A full-page newspaper advertisement lured you to start and continue looking through a series of lined-up circular objects—bottle tops of seven soft drinks, a cut-in-half orange and tomato. At the end, under a Bacardi bottle top of the same shape and size, the first part of bold copy said **Bacardi rum mixes with everything.** Then, under an automobile steering wheel of similar shape and size, it added **Except driving.** GOTCHA!

In another newspaper advertisement, under the headline "the typical executive fitness program," there were five panels. The first, labeled "Monday," showed a chubby man in a sweatsuit jogging briskly with a confident smile on his face. "Tuesday" showed him jogging quite a bit less briskly . . . with no smile. "Wednesday" showed him sagging badly. By "Thursday," he's about to collapse. On "Friday," he's *not there!* GOTCHA!

I love that Tactic, and wish we had room for more.

4. Word Play—Clever/Clear The *first* part of this Tactic title is self-explanatory. The *second* part emphasizes what I say throughout this book: OK, be clever. I love it. BUT remain clear! When a great advertisement for Mr. Coffee coffeemakers carries a headline saying **America's favorite brewery** that's clever AND clear. When a great advertisement for Hyundai, maker of low-price cars, carries a headline saying **Debt end**, that's clever AND clear. When Lipton shows a slender young girl sipping iced tea with the headline **Go skinny sippin'**, that's clever AND clear. And, from earlier chapters, do you remember **Go out and hug a road you like, Mother him on Father's Day, Buy cheap sox and pay through the toes,** and, for a rechargeable battery miniature stereo, **Why pay cash for batteries when you can charge it?** All of these are clever AND clear. All make Routine Propositions into great print advertisements by using the Creative Tactic of Word Play—Clever/Clear.

5. Acceptable Exaggeration If any king ever cried, "My kingdom for a horse!" I'm sure he would have backed down if someone had replied, "Sire, here's a horse; please give me your kingdom." Today, if we say, "I'd give my right arm for a cold beer," we sure as hell don't expect to live up to *that* deal. In literature and conversation, we allow for certain exaggerations. People allow for them in advertising, too, which gives us another fruitful Creative Tactic.

please do not lick this page!

Of course no one expected anybody to lick the page above, but this Acceptable Exaggeration made one of advertising history's great print advertisements for Life Savers.

Note that for this Tactic to work successfully, readers must instantly know you're kidding, as I knew the instant I saw an utterly charming advertisement with the Routine Proposition of "buy our marshmallows for your kids." An adorable red-headed, blue-eyed little boy, smiling conspiratorially and holding a marshmallow on a stick, stood under the headline **A marshmallow a day makes your blue eyes bluer.** Not only an acceptable but also a heart-winning and certainly meaningful attention-getting exaggeration!

6. Quick/Easy Game Recall one of the Creative Tactics for Increasing INTEREST called Proposition Challenge (**Are you man enough to do a woman's work?**). If you cannot use that Tactic, perhaps you can Increase Meaningful ATTENTION by doing your *advertisement* in the form of an easily recognized, easily played, but friendly, challenging little game. One that intrigues readers so much they simply have to try it—and, in doing so, give your Routine Proposition significantly more time than they otherwise would have—thus qualifying your work as a great or near-great print advertisement.

For its soft contact lenses, Bausch & Lomb successfully applied this technique in an advertisement showing a large leaf with what appeared to be drops of rain water sprinkled on it. The headline said: **One of these drops of water is a Bausch & Lomb soft lens. Can you find it?** You simply *had* to try, which drew significantly more than normal attention to the advertisement. And it was Increased Meaningful ATTENTION to the proposition that Bausch & Lomb soft lenses (as the copy said) **"are made with water . . . So they look like water, and [are] almost as soft."**

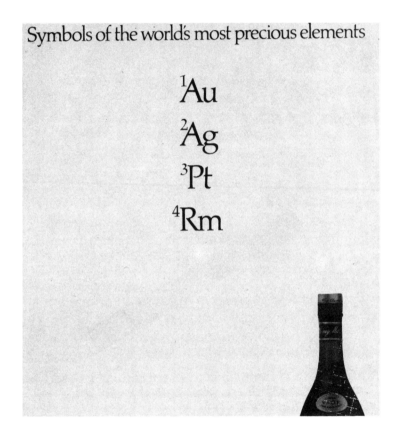

Look at this headline and the symbols under it. Can you name them? You just have to stop and try. Then you see the answers at the bottom of the page: gold, silver, platinum, and Remy Martin V.S.O.P. In playing this Quick/Easy Game, you gave the advertisement Increased Meaningful ATTENTION because you got the proposition that Remy Martin is a "precious" cognac.

7. VOILA! This is entirely an *art* Tactic, but it is one that requires you to make the art and headline work together. The headline says something, and the art makes a visually powerful and/or dramatic and/or surprising—in some way grabbing—portrayal of what the headline says.

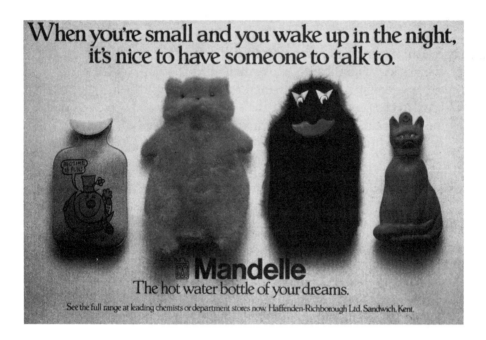

Read this headline; then glance at the pictures. VOILA! You see hot water bottles made in the shapes and textures of cuddly things kids can take to bed and talk to when they wake up in the night. Outstanding for greatly Increased Meaningful ATTENTION.

8. Vivid Visualization This Tactic is like the salesperson who jumps onto a suitcase to demonstrate its strength. Though I know Dishwasher *all* is a fine product, I have seen *other* products make this same claim. But not with the same Vivid Visualization that raises this advertisement to the great level—by getting Increased Meaningful ATTENTION for its Routine Proposition.

One of Seagram's "don't drink and drive" series of great advertisements showed the words *I can drive when I drink* handwritten five times on a page. The first time, it appears normal and is written under the words: **The party begins.** Then, under the words **2 drinks later,** the handwriting appears to be a little scrawled, as if from a less steady hand. The handwriting keeps getting more and more unsteady through **After 4 drinks, After 5 drinks** until, under **After 7 drinks in all,** it looks like the labored scribble of someone suffering from cerebral palsy. What a Vivid Visualization! What greatly Increased Meaningful ATTENTION!

These days, with computers, everyone seems to be into preparing printed presentations. And to meet the resulting demand have come *many* systems for binding such presentations. Hence, good as 3M's Scotch™ Binding System may be, it needed a way to get Increased Meaningful ATTENTION. So the top of one of its advertisements carried these words and this Vivid Visualization.

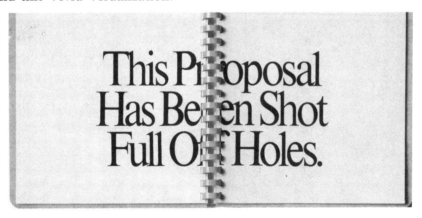

With permission of 3M

And the bottom half of the advertisement carried these words with this Vivid Visualization.

9. Hey, I'm Talking to You! The most famous, most imitated version of this Tactic first appeared not as an advertisement but as a poster for military recruiting during World War I: James Montgomery Flagg's stern Uncle Sam pointing a finger and looking directly at you with the bold words **I WANT YOU FOR U.S. ARMY.** The Quaker Oats people certainly did a marvelous take-off on that with this advertisement for Kibbles, and I doubt anyone could argue with my contention that they got Increased Meaningful ATTENTION for their Routine Proposition to buy Kibbles instead of some other dog food.

With permission of The Quaker Oats Co.

Usually, you work this Tactic by having some famous person look directly into the camera with mouth open as though speaking and with an animated "talking to you" expression on his or her face. To understand why this Tactic works, imagine yourself walking along a street, coming to a store show window, and seeing someone inside gesturing excitedly and obviously trying to talk to you. Could you pass by without stopping?

10. Kids and Dogs That could read Kids OR Dogs, and I am sure it needs no explanation, not even an illustration. If your proposition has anything to do with kids and/or dogs, or if you have any logical reason to use pictures of them, spend the money for the best casting agency and the most talented photographer. If the two produce as they should, you will have a photograph that can get increased attention for the *most* Routine Proposition with which anyone ever had to work. And if you practice what I've preached throughout this chapter, it will also get Increased *Meaningful-to-your-Proposition* ATTENTION.

(**Author's NOTE**: If you can identify another Creative Tactic, and illustrate with at least three advertisements made great by using it, I will gratefully—and, with acknowledging credit—include it in my seminars. If we do another printing of this book, I will do the same there. Meanwhile, in the next chapter, let's now look at a sampling of great print advertisements, along with explanations of exactly what makes them great.)

Sampling of Great Print Advertisements and What Made Them Great

13

For over 30 years now, I have tried to stimulate the creating of more great print advertisements by giving a unique Print Award for "excellence in print advertising." Unique because advertisements do not *"win"* the award. They *earn* it. I critique them with over 80 questions and requirements relating to all we have covered in this book (and which you will find for your use in the Appendix). *Only* those advertisements that get all "YES" answers in the CHECKLIST part and score straight 10s in the method/artistry (SCORING SYSTEM) part earn the Print Award.

The photograph on page 192 shows two 1969 Print Award earners, Shirley Polykoff and Eric Lundun of Foote, Cone & Belding, for the great **Does she . . . or doesn't she?** Clairol campaign.

Obviously, I hope this entire book helps produce always Effective and more often Great Print Advertisements. And I hope this chapter—by showing and citing only a very small sampling of truly Great Print Advertisements—inspires and stimulates. But, throughout my years of work, especially as an eager young hopeful listening to the "greats," I have lamented—and gone away unhelped by—urgings that were lyrically written and spoken but empty of "how to" guidance, thus useless: "dare to be different," "reach for the moon," "break the rules," and the like. I mention this as a lead-in to saying that I hope you find any inspiration I give you accompanied by *concrete help in how to fulfill it.*

In my explanations of why each advertisement ranks as great, you will find part of what I write applying to *that* advertisement only. But you will also see that I sing some of the *same* praises for every one, which reflects the fact that great print advertisements *all have certain aspects and elements in common.*

"CHIVAS on the rocks."

Advertiser: Chivas Regal
Agency: DDB Needham

"CHIVAS on the rocks," orders an ordinary-looking fellow at the end of the bar. Next to him, another man who could be an identical twin indiscriminately orders just "Scotch on the rocks." And next to him another look-alike gives an equally haphazard order of "Scotch on the rocks." Two more do the same: "Scotch on the rocks." "Scotch on the rocks." Then the beautiful lady asks, "Bartender, who's that attractive man at the end of the bar?" GOTCHA!

What a magnificent execution of that Creative Tactic! And magnificently supported by a perceptively-*planned* and courageous—yes, *courageous*—advertisement. Few advertisers would have had the courage to run with neither headline nor "closing copy." (I can imagine the questions of the timid: "You *can't* run an ad without a headline, can you?" "Shouldn't we end with some explanation? Shouldn't we run a block of copy? Suppose people don't *get* it?") But this client and agency obviously (and astutely) understood that, with a headline across the top, or with the "ady" sight of a copy block or blocks, they would *not* have lured people into reading this great advertisement *before deciding to start.* Which means the GOTCHA! Tactic would not have worked so smoothly. And as for explaining the "joke"— bless both the Chivas and DDB Needham people for their Noel Coward forbearance.

I know the Chivas Regal Proposition well. Yet this great advertisement not only got me to recall it once again but also made me *want* to because I so enjoyed the delivery. This demonstrates that, in tone, the advertisement understood me. Also, it went with the tide because I believe most all people are prepared to accept the Chivas proposition. And it surely got to the point.

Finally, note these details of solid and smart execution: the precisely right type style and setting for easy readability and for "dialogue." (A traditional serif face set u&lc and roman) The drop-out of all background, which accentuates the men's similar appearance, sets up the man-to-man-to-man-to-man-to-man sequence and (critically important) sets *off* the *difference*—red dress (in the full-color original) and femininity—of the final figure.

While this great advertisement was running, I wish I had asked a bartender how many men had recently put an elbow on the bar, a suave look on their faces, and ordered, "CHIVAS on the rocks." *Then* looked expectantly to the other end of the bar.

"Something tells me you have a cat."

With permission of S. C. Johnson & Son, Inc.

Advertiser: S. C. Johnson & Son
Agency: Foote, Cone & Belding

Other products that fill "cat boxes" make the same claim as Litter Fresh does. Yet this advertisement went immediately into my collection of print greats as a perfect execution of *two* tried and proved Creative Tactics. It follows approach 2-C on our Creative Flow Chart, using a *combination* of Tactics to both Increase INTEREST and Increase Meaningful ATTENTION: **Heaven Forbid!** and **Oh, I Get It.**

Heaven Forbid! Recall that the Proposition relates to something people want to avoid, and the Tactic magnifies the consequences of it happening. Imagine your mortification if a houseguest wrinkled a nose with distaste and said this headline! Heaven forbid! What would you do to avoid that embarrassment? Use Litter Fresh? Yes!

Oh, I Get It! The major art and the headline "act out" the Proposition. You "get it," and feel so delighted with yourself that you will be long, if ever, in forgetting what you "got" from this great print advertisement. (A related, but separate, element of greatness in this advertisement is the recognition that Litter Fresh could not explicitly describe the problem and remain in good taste. Thus, the use of the Creative Tactic is both brilliant and necessary.)

In execution of the basics, as with all great advertisements, it makes not a single mistake.

No mistake of using a *photograph* of a real nose wrinkled in distaste—how ugly! Or a photographed real nose detached from its face—how grotesque! Rather, by using artwork, with just a slight tilt of the nostrils and a small line on the bridge, an actually *pleasant*—sort of a Santa Claus—nose says it all.

No mistake in typography. Readers *expect* to see words within quotes set in a traditional serif face and u&lc. You can *hear* this headline "speaking."

No mistake of laboring the point. Even people who have no personal experience with cats can instantly understand the message. People at whom it is aimed—cat owners—feel acutely sensitive to the problem. No need, then, to make *readers'* noses wrinkle by describing it. Enough to ask, in essence, "Got this problem?" and to advise, "Then try this product."

No mistake of over-promising. The copy later says Litter Fresh *virtually* eliminates odors. Nothing enhances believability more than a touch of understatement.

Does this advertisement go with the tide (in this case, with what people want to avoid)? Does it get to the point? Does it understand people? I don't need "something" to tell me—this great advertisement speaks for itself!

"My insurance company?
New England Life, of course. Why?"

Advertiser: New England Mutual Life
Agency: Hill, Holliday, Connors, Cosmopulos

I salute this representative of a great advertising campaign first of all for its brilliant solution to a dilemma faced by all advertisers of life insurance policies: To present the Propositional Benefit, they cannot avoid reminding us of our mortality. How then to present it while staying *entirely away* from scare tactics? Well, we believe *homo sapiens* is the only species that lives with the knowledge that someday we must die. But surely we are also the only living creatures with such a sense of humor that we can *joke about it*. Ah, but we make a *distinction* between those jokes about death that make us laugh and those that make us flinch and turn away because they "hit too close to home." In the deftly demonstrated understanding of that phrase—"too close to home"—we find the genius of this series of great print advertisements: The sensitive perception that one form of "acceptable" humor on the subject is to depict a life-threatening situation *entirely unlikely ever to occur*. That sensitive perception directed this client and agency to a Creative Tactic that provides opportunity for such depiction: Acceptable Exaggeration:

> "*My insurance company? New England Life, of course. Why?*"
> "*Because you are about to be skewered by a 1,250-pound swordfish!*"
> "*Really?*"
> "*No, not really . . . we're just exaggerating to make a point.*"
> [Pun intended.]

It always impresses me that, when you find a perfectly executed advertisement, it seems the *only* way to have done it. But consider that, for illustrations, most advertising people think first and most naturally of *photography*. Thus, for this advertisement, a *discerning* mind had to think differently. For two reasons, only a cartoon-type rendering would work: (1) Only a drawing could possibly depict the scene and (2) only a cartoon, which instantly signals humor, could carry it off. (And added laurels for the superb decision to hire the talented Rowland B. Wilson because his inimitable style goes beyond the normally strong ability of any cartoon and caption to attract the eye.) Finally, regarding the caption, note the use of THE most easily readable type style and setting. My insurance advertising best? New England Life, of course.

Now there's a Dove that smells like this.

Advertiser: Lever Brothers
Agency: Ogilvy & Mather

As we have, noted, when marketing provides a great proposition, the route to great advertising directs us to simply make the great proposition quickly, easily, and fully clear—leaving it to the content of the great proposition to make it memorable.

But, *if* you can add one of the Creative Tactics to increase interest or meaningful attention—and do it *without losing one iota of clarity*—you make an advertisement that has the power of a rocket with booster engine. And Ogilvy & Mather's creative crew gave Unscented Dove exactly such a boosted launching.

Having market researched a growing demand for un-scented products, Lever gave the agency a great proposition in developing and offering Unscented Dove. And a straight announcement would have made many readers pause and read. But by writing the headline "Now there's a Dove that smells like this" and placing it over two blank pages—over *nothing:*

- Without question, the empty pages where readers expect to find words and pictures made many more readers pause/stop (many more than would have for a straight delivery of the great proposition).
- The combination of that headline over the very quick curiosity-arousing and equally quick curiosity-*satisfying* blank pages artistically execute the Creative Tactic of "Oh, I Get It!" And, because people "figured it out for themselves," that gave the Dove announcement extra impact and memorability.

As with all totally great print advertisements, the artistry rests on a foundation of flawless basics. In this great one, note, from top to bottom:

The Typography: We noted earlier that eyes generally go first to an illustration, but here the "illustration" is blank space. So eyes go first to the headline. Which means that if the head and art must work together in a quick, one-two sequence, the headline *must* be so easy to read that people do it before they realize it. Half of that will depend upon the type style and setting, and (as you find me repeating) you simply cannot do better than use a traditional serif face set u&lc roman.

The Writing: The other half will depend upon the writing, and you simply cannot do better than use familiar words in familiar sequence.

The Layout: As I write, I don't know how the advertise-ment will reproduce in black and white in this book, but, in magazines, I'll wager that people would say they saw two *entirely white* pages. But the product *box* is white. Thus, as a final demonstration of thoroughly professional execution, a subtle graying of the lower right corner made the white package stand out.

If you asked me to list the flaws in the execution of this great print advertisement, I would hand you a sheet of blank paper.

Finished! In half the time.

With permission of Minwax Co., Inc.

Advertiser: Minwax Company
Agency: Gilbert Whitney & Johns

Marketing used the product position and advertising used—brilliantly—the Creative Tactic of "You Can Do It ...Easily" to take a Routine Proposition to print advertising greatness. But I know that this great print advertisement would *never* win any typical advertising-juried award. My Gawd, where is the cleverness? If they—those juries—could recognize *true* cleverness and true professionalism, they would find evidence of these qualities throughout this page.

As readers' eyes first see it, what must the advertisement signal instantly? Its subject: *Finishing unpainted furniture.* Look at that big, beautifully finished chest of drawers made extra bold and recognizable by silhouetting it, not diffusing its outline by showing it in a furnished room. And can you possibly look at the finished chest without seeing—simultaneously—the same chest *unfinished?* (With *that* chest revealing another smart and fine touch: "no drawer pulls" making "*un*finished" even more clear.)

What must the advertisement say about finishing furniture with Minwax Polyshades? *That the product lets you finish furniture faster.* Look at the Polyshades can with the brush pointing to the word "Finished!" And you cannot possibly see that word without seeing—simultaneously—the words "In half the time." This is what happens when you skillfully stack very short lines one over the other: Readers can (and do) see and read more than one line at a time (here, three), especially when you use such an exceptionally easy-to-read typeface, set so bold and u&lc roman. And did you ever see a leg—just *part* of a leg—say so much so fast as does that of the departing young lady? It is dungareed, yes, but the four-color original showed a yellow sock and red sneaker—a do-it-yourselfer leg if I ever saw one—and that adds a repeat of "easy" to the message.

What else must the advertisement say? That the product has reduced an ordinarily two-step job to *one* step. From the last line of the read-at-a-glance headline, you slide right into set-for-easiest-reading copy: "Polyshades is stain and polyurethane in one. So you get beautiful color and tough protection in the same stroke." *Reader's Digest* editors could not have said as much in any fewer words. I will finish this citation without mentioning the clever double-meaning of a key word in the headline.

FALSE/TRUE

Advertiser: General Foods USA
Agency: Ogilvy & Mather

"Play *hard*ball, but don't get rough" could have been the instructions to those who created this great print advertisement . . . with a detailed translation of that being:

- Admit that fried chicken tastes great.
- Don't preach about fried chicken soaking up fat, but still, somehow, "say" that it does.
- Offer the great taste of fried chicken with*out* frying, and "say" that baking covers chicken with "goodness."

The greatness of this advertisement comes, in part, from the deftness with which it follows these instructions and, in the process, expertly uses the Creative Tactic of "OK Competitiveness." (With overtones of "It's OK To Do." and "Vivid Visualization.")

It does not label as FALSE the universally known *fact* that fried chicken tastes great, but rather the *belief* that frying is the only route to that great taste. It does not explicitly condemn fried chicken as loaded with cholesterol, but a reader would have to be blind and oblivious to the cholesterol problem not to come near gagging at the sight of all that bubbling, splattering oil in the ironware skillet (the overtone of "Vivid Visualization").

Readers would also have to be blind not to "taste" the appetite appeal of the golden-brown, crisp (and seemingly greaseless) pieces of chicken so deliciously illustrating the statement: "Great Tasting Chicken Can Be Prepared Without Frying." And, finally, they would have to be insensitive to the fine use of words not to see the health connotation in the word "goodness" in the tagline "THANK GOODNESS FOR SHAKE 'N BAKE" (the overtone of "It's OK To Do"). Give the advertisement honors, then, for its positive strength achieved without being coarsely negative.

Now, add Magna to the honors for (1) the handsomely stark, single-illustration pages, (2) the bold "FALSE/ TRUE," and (3) the terse overlines. For these three elements of execution make an advertisement you cannot possibly pass by. And then, having stopped readers, these same three elements deliver the message—fully and with powerful impact—in *six seconds flat!* Now, to a quality common to all great advertisements (getting to the point), add two others: going with the tide and understanding people. (Anticholesterol goes with the tide, and pro-the-taste of fried chicken certainly understands people.)

What do I, an advocate of traditional serif typefaces, think of the typography? I *repeat* that, for certain words (here, TRUE and FALSE) I would use nothing *but* all-caps sans serif. And for nearby short lines of copy, to avoid an abutting inconsistency in type "weights," I would use nothing *but* a good, same-weight, round, open sans serif set u&lc roman exactly as the makers of this great print advertisement did. (And exactly as I would expect from this advertiser and agency, both masters of print advertising.)

Instead of trying to give your car a personality . . .

With permission of American Honda Motor Co. Inc. via Rubin Postaer

Advertiser: Honda Civic
Agency: Rubin Postaer and Associates

I suspect that few clients would believe an agency promise to produce a print advertisement that would get people to spend maybe 10 to 20 minutes studying the advertisement, *enjoying* it thoroughly, and, in the process, *getting the proposition repeatedly.* But I expect the Honda people *did* believe such a promise, for certainly by now they must have come to expect print miracles from Gerry Rubin, Larry Postaer, and their extraordinarily talented Associates.

My wife did not know that I admire this agency and the advertising they do for Honda. Hence it was entirely the appeal of this great advertisement that prompted her to call out with a chuckle, "Look at *this!*" and then to sit with me—spending time with an *advertisement*—both of us completely drawn in and held by the *expert* execution of the Creative Tactic "Quick/Easy Game."

- Expert because vanity plate by vanity plate, it was quick; but the spread showed so many plates, in total we gave it far more attention than we have ever given any advertisement, and we ended up wanting *more*. Just as when you are "getting" the words of a crossword puzzle, when you are happily "winning" the "Quick/Easy Game," you can't get enough.
- Expert also because, while each little "puzzle" challenged us enough to make it fun, they were easy enough to give us *repeated* victories of solution. (Rubin Postaer clearly knew that the "Game" Tactic would not work if it took too long to get only *one* solution.)
- Expert still more because the plates at upper left, where, of course, you start, are among the easiest. Immediately, my wife and I had EIEIO, then BRBDL, then IMWHOIM (perfect for an independent Down Easter from Maine), and by then we were hooked into giving whatever time it took to get the likes of EYEMA10 (I hope he or she was), YRU-NVS, and the laid-back ABDABDO. See what I mean?

But...BUT...remember my caution about getting so caught up with executing the game that you forget the proposition. *Not these people.* Their proposition: A Civic is fun, with a perky *personality* you can love. My wife and I got that proposition with each plate we solved, for all the while we kept seeing the advertisement's only line: **Instead of trying to give your car a personality, maybe you should try a car that already comes with one. The Civic Hatchback.** This line was set, as are all Rubin Postaer advertisements I've ever seen, in an easy-reading traditional serif u&lc roman. (And, yes, for a combination headline/copy not intended to be read at a glance, one long line makes the right typographic "floor" for this layout.)

IR8ITGR8!

HE WAS never elected. But every night...

HE WAS never elected. But every night "Mayor" Orlo McBain is the last man to walk the streets of Culross, Scotland. He checks a knob, closes a gate and goes his way. The good things in life stay that way.

Preferred for smoothness, Dewar's® never varies.

"White Label"
DEWAR'S,
BLENDED SCOTCH WHISKY
100% SCOTCH WHISKIES
PRODUCT OF SCOTLAND

With permission of Schenley Industries, Inc.

Advertiser: Schenley Imports
Agency: Leo Burnett

In the blue-light cast of early evening, a cap-wearing, tweed-jacketed old man walks with his collie on the cobbled streets of what seems a Northern European village — such is the light and the style of the houses. A ring of obviously old brass keys pull our eyes to **HE WAS never elected. But every night "Mayor" Orlo McBain is the last man to walk the streets of Culross, Scotland. He checks a knob, closes a gate and goes his way. The good things in life stay that way.**

Before you knew it, didn't you read it through to the end? And see there the White Label bottle? And with it **Preferred for smoothness, Dewar's® never varies**? How could anyone not? And in the reading not recall again how Dewar's has been with us for aye ... and always with the same smoothness on the tongue?

What *artistry* in the execution of the Creative Tactic of "Short Short Story"! How effective the Tactic, when thus applied, in getting a so-oft repeated, hence by now Routine Proposition perceived as one of "The good things in life ... " Not just another scotch whisky, but something interwoven like a warm color through the tartan of living.

And what absolute *competence* in the execution of the basics! Recall with me (from Chapter 8) the requirements for an advertisement without a headline, and note the total adherence to them here:

- The text must be set very large—around 18 to 24 points. *And this measures a wee bit more than 24.*
- You must lay out the copy so that eyes go first and naturally to the beginning and flow easily through it. *Those keys pull your eyes to the first words, and it is simply straight across and down short lines from there.*
- You must use an extraordinarily easy-reading typeface, set in an equally easy-to-read way. *And here a classic traditional serif face, with short ascenders/descenders leaving generously large bodies, set u&lc roman and black on light gray. Textbook!*
- You must write short, easy-to-scan-understand, sentences. *Remember, "short" is relative, and even one 17-word sentence in the copy "reads short" and is understood at sight.*
- The "story-line" must flow smoothly and in a straight, easy-to-follow sequence with no detours. *Straight through you go, with all of it flowing as smoothly as the whisky.*

A steaming haggis for these lads and lassies, and another round to toast them with!

What others ask . . . What Goodyear asks

Advertiser: Goodyear
Agency: Young & Rubicam

A print advertisement can prove itself great by taking—with outstanding success—a sequence of steps, starting the instant it is exposed to readers. First, as readers turn pages (so often with their minds "elsewhere"), something in or about the advertisement must capture their attention to make them pause. In this great print advertisement, the two stark and bold circles created by the no-background side view of the tires do that job superbly, pulling readers' eyes to the pages with the graphic power of a double Cyclops.

Second, the advertisement must be so skillfully written, laid out, and typographically composed that readers will—still with no effort—immediately see or sense a reason to *turn their pause into a stop* and their attention to *interest*. Initially, the reason can be simply to satisfy curiosity, but satisfaction of curiosity must lead immediately to a more *meaningful* benefit. Here, at first sight, readers sense more than simple satisfaction of curiosity; they see *benefit in the satisfaction of it*. For they identify a tire advertisement but not the cliché cross section of tire construction, tire gripping wet pavement, or over-wide tread. Instead, they see the impossible-to-miss (thus automatically read) headline words "buy a tire" on *both* pages and the two small pieces of copy with the tire at left contrasting with the many more with the tire at right. This contrast signals two different approaches to buying, and these elements add the promise of *"learning something useful"* to satisfaction of curiosity.

Third—and without this no greatness—the advertisement must communicate its proposition in a way that serves *both* readers (else why should they read it?) *and* advertiser (else why run it?). This advertisement serves *readers* by (1) providing the many-more-than-size/price questions that should be asked and answered to buy wisely. And by (2) identifying the tire-maker who asks and answers these questions for the benefit of buyers. It serves the *advertiser* with a straight-10 execution of the Creative Tactic for Greatness: "Go Beyond Product Features." This does not claim for Goodyear tires materials, design, or workmanship that others can and do also boast. Rather, it positions Goodyear as the tire company that cares seriously about fitting you with exactly the right tires for your car. Repeatedly and consistently so positioned with such great advertisements as this, Goodyear will join the select few companies that profit from long-owned, unique—and unassailable—positions.

Finally—and different from what others ask in judging advertisements—included in what I ask is perfection in the basics. And, for this great job, straight 10s there, too.

MORE BRANS. GREAT TASTE.

With permission of Ralston Purina Co. via Avrett, Free & Ginsberg

Advertiser: Ralston Purina
Agency: Avrett, Free & Ginsberg

When the benefits of bran were first revealed, simply the word "bran" in a headline caught attention and interest. No longer. In fact, with so many products headlining the inclusion of bran, even a Great Proposition of not one but *four* brans in a product could easily go unnoticed. So the Ralston Purina people had to approach the Great Proposition of Multi Bran Chex as a *Routine* Proposition— and search for the Creative Tactic that would get it Increased Meaningful ATTENTION. Trust these consistently and extraordinarily good print advertisers (client and agency) to find the Tactic and then to use it in such a way as to give the word "simplicity" a new and powerful meaning.

They wanted to tell people that Multi Bran Chex contains corn, wheat, oats, and rice. And so they *simply* showed grains of those four brans and nothing else, save, at the end, the box in which they come (critically important in this supermarket self-service age). They wanted people to give Increased Meaningful ATTENTION to their proposition. So they *simply* placed bold plus signs between each grain and an equal sign before the package—producing a visually dominant and absolutely irresistible "Quick/Easy Game." Only a brain completely lacking in curiosity cells could pass without stopping to work out the quick/easy— but so propositionally meaningful—equation.

And, as always with great advertising, the method and artistry build from an execution of the basics so "right" that, once done, it seems there could have been *no other way*. You can't see it in this black-and-white reproduction, but the original glowed with golden color coming from the grains and had a buff background with a rich-brown ink for the letters and symbols. You *can* see the easy-reading serif typeface, with the all-caps appropriately used for the few headline words and u&lc right for the closing lines.

And a standing ovation for the decision to make it a horizontal half-spread—the advertisement stretching across the bottom of two pages with editorial columns above it— instead of the more normal full, vertical page. The editorial columns above it tracked eyes *into* the advertisement with the end of each column. And, during one or more of those times, this great print advertisement was one easy and natural eye-sweep from left to right.

Multi Bravos for Multi Bran Chex!

Go on, cut. You'll be brilliant . . .

Go on, cut. You'll be brilliant.
Armstrong guarantees it.

Install your new Armstrong sheet vinyl floor with a Trim and Fit ™
kit, and if you goof while cutting or fitting, your Armstrong retailer
will replace both the flooring and the kit.

Free. That's the Fail-Safe ™ Guarantee. Just see your local home
center or building supply retailer for details.

FREE. For a free Floor Project Planning Pack, call
the Armstrong Consumer Line at 1 800 233-3823 and
ask for Dept. 79GRD. Or, send this coupon:
Armstrong, Dept. 79GRD, P.O. Box 3001, Lancaster, PA 17604

Name _____
(please print)
Street _____
City _____
State _____ Zip _____

Armstrong
so nice to come home to ™

Advertiser: Armstrong
Agency: BBDO

We know, as well as know ourselves, that poor apprehensive fellow who must—sooner or later—cut into the brand-new floor covering. Because we have *been there*. And, oh, how we wish, when we were, that a trusted name such as Armstrong had assured us (1) we would do fine, but (2) if we did make a miscut, it would not spell catastrophe.

Thus, since the quintessence of marketing is to make available what people very much want (i.e., to make a Great Proposition), this great advertisement was sired by great marketing. But great marketing does not automatically produce great advertisements. For that happy sequel, the advertising people must, as the BBDO people clearly did, make a pragmatically professional observation followed by thoroughly professional creative decisions.

The observation: They had a Great Proposition to make. And one drawing its appeal from the same source as a known Creative tactic: "You Can Do It . . . Easily."

The creative decisions: Let nothing get in the way of making the Great Proposition quickly, easily, fully clear. Then add *memorability* by working for all it is worth the emotion in the "You Can Do It . . . Easily" Tactic.

Give this advertisement just 15 seconds, and you must admire how fully they achieve the objective of quick, clear, and full communication. Now note how they added memorability through the artful use of the emotion in the Tactic:

- The fine empathy revealed by the artwork, which shows such sensitive understanding of the worried man with the gleaming-sharp cutting knife in one hand and paid-for floor covering under "foot." Particularly note the discerning decision to make the illustration a drawing, not a photograph—thereby permitting the husband's perspiring anxiety to be portrayed not grimly but with warm and affectionate humor. And, borrowing from familiar comic strip technique, the use of a *dashed* line to indicate the multi-angled cut *not yet made*. In reality, of course, the man would mark an intended cut with a solid line.

- And, as always, note THE most easily readable type style and setting.

Did it happen, we wonder that when the agency showed copy and layout, the client said, "Go on, run it. You'll be brilliant. We guarantee it." Let's say it did.

Maybe it's time you lost your wallet.

We can think of several reasons to lose your wallet. Its age, condition and style for starters.

But perhaps the best reason is a new Rolfs wallet.

You see, a Rolfs wallet makes handling your financial affairs more enjoyable, because it helps keep things where they belong. Organized. Safe. At your fingertips.

And Rolfs makes over 100 different styles for men and women. So there's a wallet or clutch to fit your needs and lifestyle. In a color and style that's attractive for you.

But what makes a

Maybe it's time you lost your wallet.

Rolfs wallet most attractive is the way it's made. With real leather. So it not only lasts longer, it gets softer and better looking with age. And look at the details. The seams are skived (which means the leather is shaved slightly at the inside of the fold), so they lay flatter and look neater. The stitching is all uniform. And the clasps and zippers are strong.

We admit the thought of losing your wallet is unsettling to say the least.

But considering what you'll find in your new Rolfs wallet, you're really not losing anything at all. ROLFS Good Things Last.

Rolfs makes over 100 styles of men's and women's wallets.

With permission of Rolfs

Advertiser: Rolfs
Agency: Clarity Coverdale Rueff

Did you know that, in some of the less savory old-time carnivals, barkers in cahoots with pickpockets would warn the crowd to look out for such thieves. Which, of course, promptly made all the listeners touch, thus locate for the pickpockets, where they kept their wallets. Fortunately I was alone when I read the headline of this great print advertisement, for that is precisely what I did. Just before I laughed . . . and loved it . . . and went on to read the copy. (And doing it so easily through the impeccable typography and layout.)

On the Creative Flow Chart, this starts with a Routine Proposition: Maybe it's time you bought a new wallet. From there does it go on to reveal the three qualities common to all great print advertisements?

Does it go with the tide? How long have you had your wallet? Long enough for it to look like a worn-out shoe? If you are a man, is it an overthick, disorganized mess of old business cards and telephone numbers, with customer copies of charge slips, receipts for taxi rides and parking, etc., etc.? If a woman, how about a packed-in mess of redeemable coupons, pictures of the kids, recipes you tore out in the doctor's waiting room, etc., etc.? And, the nub of going with the tide, have you been *meaning* to buy a new and better organized wallet for a long time?

Does it understand and like people? If you, as I did, had to answer yes to all those questions above, they understand you and me (and I'm sure we can multiply us by millions). And we knew the headline was joshing—we felt it a friendly advertisement.

Ah, but does it get to the point? Actually, the pictures of the old and new wallets and the headline *do* make the point in seconds: Time to buy a new wallet. Then the length of the copy signals that they have facts to give on why you might want to buy a Rolfs wallet. And, after all this time, a new wallet is not something you will just buy without thinking, right? So this is one of the advertisements that signals it will get to the point, but deliberately not fast (and you don't want it to).

Finally, with a Routine Proposition, does it use expertly one of the Creative Tactics to Increase INTEREST or Meaningful ATTENTION? Well, I was not even thinking of this book when I just spontaneously thought, "Oh, I Get It!"

For 50 years, our greatest invention . . .

With permission of 3M

Advertiser: Commercial Tape Division/3M
Agency: Martin Williams Advertising

Proof, indeed, we have here that great advertisements live a long, long time. 3M's Commercial Tape Division could at this writing change that "50" to "62," make absolutely no other changes, and run this advertisement again—and have it acclaimed again as great. Yes, I have had this great advertisement, have admired and used it for a full dozen years now! Used it in a seminar module in which I show some 75 advertisements that all shine with the three qualities common to great print advertisements, all take their right routes to greatness, and all use with consumate skill—and that touch of artistry—precisely the right Creative Tactic.

Consider these points about this terse but total use of the Tactic "Oh, I Get It!"

I repeated only a few pages ago that eyes always go to the illustration first. But for this great print advertisement, they worked to keep that from happening—and succeeded. They made the headline the visually strongest element on the page, so your eyes go *there* first, and you scan-read 10 words that arouse your curiousity—as this Tactic must. But recall, too, that, in advertising, curiosity aroused must signal the *benefit of curiosity quickly satisfied*. The sight of only one more line on the page ensures that, and you read, **"Scotch® Brand Transparent Tape is 50 years old."** And when your eyes reach that word "old" they see the familiar tartan tab, and now—only *now*—your eyes move up from it diagonally and you note the hard to see . . . *deliberately* hard to see "greatest invention," the Scotch Tape! You get the play between headline and illustration, and, in the process, you have given Increased Meaningful ATTENTION to a Routine Proposition.

Increased *Meaningful* ATTENTION because the headline/illustration play adroitly and dramatically makes the Proposition point. *Of course* "virtually unnoticed." Precisely why we use Scotch Tape in so many ways when we want the adhesion of tape but want also to see through it.

For the three qualities common to all great advertisements, I say, "Yes, yes, yes." And in marking "the basics," all 10s, specifically for the typography, of course, but also for the breaking of the headline into short, vertical "takes," and (though you cannot see it here) the selection of a medium brown background, which made the tape transparent as it should be but visible when you looked more carefully to "get it."

There are less expensive bourbons...

Advertiser: Austin Nichols Distilling
Agency: Angotti, Thomas, Hedge

I feel grateful for *all* great print advertisements—grateful simply because they were done. I feel *additional* gratitude for this one because it provides such a clear and *instructive* movement through the Creative Flow Chart from a Routine Proposition to unquestioned greatness. (I noted earlier and think it is worth repeating here: A proposition can remain as justified as ever but become Routine from repetition and/or—as in this case—from the fact that every higher-priced product can and does propose: "Pay more for the best." *Though none that I know of have ever made that proposition with such pithy and delightful—thus acceptable—impudence.*)

Where this work moves next—to the three parts and qualities of all great advertisements—provides a perfect example and opportunity to reemphasize a point about the first quality: *In Content, Go With The Tide.* The point is that we have *many* tides flowing "out there," and creating a great print advertisement demands discerning and going with the *right* one for its proposition—as Wild Turkey does in turning its higher price *to advantage* by going with the tide of those who want and will pay for thicker steaks and bigger cars—whether or not they *normally* do. (See "masterstroke" below.)

In the first paragraph on this citation, I call this copy "pithy." For "pithy," read "Get To The Point"—the second quality common to all great print advertisements. Also, I referred to its "delightful—thus *acceptable*—impudence." For that, read "Understands and Likes People"—the third quality.

Next, under Creative Approach, I see the *master-stroke* in selecting the route through "Logic." Because those willing to pay more for the best will, of course, find this headline entirely logical. But, think about it, even those who ordinarily *must* settle for thinner steaks and smaller cars find it *equally logical,* which means that this advertisement goes not only with the *demo*graphic tide of those who can afford to and always *do* "buy the best" but also with the *psycho*graphic tide of those who *want* to—and when the price difference amounts to relatively few dollars, occasionally do. As I am sure this great advertisement spurred many to do.

In this textbook move through the Flow Chart, we applaud the use of the Creative Strategy of seeking Increased Meaningful INTEREST. We both chortle and cheer for the magnificent use of the Creative Tactic: "Yes, That's True." (And on top of all that, the strong and clear Voice of Print created by the perfectly selected and set type.)

PUT A LITTLE MORE IN YOUR POCKET . . .

PUT A LITTLE MORE IN YOUR POCKET...

Suppose we said you could save a little money while you did a little something for the environment. Interested?

We thought you'd be. So we created the Downy® Refill with a full 64 ounces of fluffy softness and freshness. But it comes in a much smaller package.

AND A LITTLE LESS IN YOUR GARBAGE.

That means there's less trash to throw away, so there's less waste building up in the environment. And the Refill is as easy to use as it is economical. Just pour it into a 64 ounce Downy® bottle and add water. In April Fresh and SunRinse Fresh, too. Was saving money ever simpler? Or better for our environment?

Less Money.* Less Waste.

*The Downy® Refill costs less per use than regular Downy.

Advertiser: Procter & Gamble
Agency: Grey Advertising

I can sense no disagreement when I write, as I have earlier and do now, that the bedrock science, skill, and art of successful marketing and advertising lies in *thoroughly understanding people*. In knowing, to the most subtle nuance, what people want and then finding a way to profit by providing it.

By that accepted standard, examine—and admire as I do—the work of both client and agency here: P&G with its renowned down-to-earthness, probably needed little research to visualize and empathize with:

- People pouring out the last ounce of Downy and then having another large plastic container to dispose of.
- People feeling the discomforting sense of recession—in some cases, worse—and gravitating to ways of saving quarters, dimes, and even nickels.

And, typical of these astute marketers, P&G pragmatized that earnings come from selling Downy, *not* its container. Enter Downy Refill—Downy less the water, economically and compactly packaged. And now enter the equally pragmatic *advertising* thinking, notable for the resulting discipline as well as for artistically applied methodology.

Recognizing a Great Proposition when they saw one, these complete and totally professional advertising practitioners took the proved route to greatness: straightforward illustration and explanation, disciplining away any possible distraction from quick, easy, fully clear presentation of the Proposition. But, while remaining Factual and Creatively NON-Creative, the agency reached out from that route to use a Creative Tactic to Increase Meaningful ATTENTION: "Vivid Visualization."

In the execution, I admire the use of a seamless-white background, leaving all the white space above and thus adding impact to the compacted package. I admire the rhythm of the two-part headline, with its familiar combinations of words in familiar sequence. In the "product shot" at bottom, I admire putting the carton next to the regular plastic container to show its size. I admire the honest and disarming perspective in the copy, in proposing to "save a *little* money" and do "a *little* something for the environment." I admire the typography, the hint of serifs that softens (how appropriate for Downy) the headline—and, yes, I might use all caps for such short lines.

In total, how much do I admire this work? Easily more than enough to place it where I doubt any typical advertising jury would: among the greats.

Ours are made to start the first time.

Ours are made to start first time.
Our comp...
Our compompomp...
Our compompompompet...
Our compompompompetitors...

Our new range of spark plugs fit British and foreign ma kes of car. **Thousands of parts for millions of cars.** **UNIPART**

Advertiser: Unipart Group of Companies
Agency: Saatchi & Saatchi Advertising (London)

Citing and backgrounding this utterly superb print advertisement leads me to start with what can come off as only the *expected* from a life-long print evangelist who deplores the pouring of tons of money (much of it wasted) into television advertising. But I must observe that this is why, during the period in which this advertisement appeared, the British were doing so much more great print advertisements than we Americans were. I don't believe this is the case now. But, while in London doing a series of seminars, I asked my UK agency friends why it was then. I must admit to a moment of regretting I had asked when they so readily and enthusiastically agreed that they did indeed do "so *much* better than you colonials." But the rest of the answer made sense: "We don't have clients who throw so much money at television. We work harder at print and put our best people on it." (This echoes what has happened here in the United States with liquor advertising.)

I can see that, but also more: They *own* the language. They seem to delight in working with it . . . in *playing* with it. Also, I believe most of them get a better liberal arts, that is, a better *literary* education than we do. It took me ten minutes to look up and learn how to *spell* "onomatopoeia," and I doubt I would *ever* have thought of using it in advertising. But look at it! It starts with a proposition so routine I cannot imagine a spark plug that does not make it. Yet it roars to greatness with this magnificent execution—this *unique* execution—of what (I hope) is now a familiar Creative Tactic to you: "Oh, I Get It!" (coming through the Creative Approach of "OK Competitiveness").

Does it go with the tide? Who wants spark plugs that start the car the first time? Does it get to the point? I "got it" by the third line . . . and went on simply for the fun of it. Does it understand and like people? Any advertisement that makes me laugh while making its point gets a "yes" from me. Also, I say "yes, yes, yes" to a bold *sans* serif face— for pompompomp engine sounds (not dialogue). Stacked exactly as you see it, the copy gives you a visual as well as verbal "depiction" of the engine that will not start.

This advertisement was made to be great the first and every time!

CODA
How to
Always Get
At Least
90% of the Way
to Greatness . . .
and More Often All the Way

I drew an analogy between going for the gold in figure skating and going for greatness in advertising.

First, the Compulsories

In skating, we cannot win the gold unless we score very high in the compulsories. In advertising, we cannot reach greatness unless we score *perfectly* in the compulsories—there is no reason for mistakes in the basics. I offered as print advertising compulsories **The A, B & C of Effective Print Advertising**.

A. Regarding "this product at this time," the advertisement must start where people are to offer the strongest possible product benefit (The Propositional Benefit) to the largest number of the right people. And the visually strongest—thus, first seen—element of the advertisement *must* be compatible with that Propositional Benefit. At this point, it's as though the reader has come upon something of interest to him or her, and, while the visually strongest element may or may not define that interest immediately—given only an idle, mind-absent glance, it *must not* camouflage or obfuscate the content or nature of that interest in any way.

B. Given that idle, mind-absent glance, the advertisement must signal *some* reason for readers to *pause*—by means of its overall "look," the style or content of an illustration, or key words in the headline. It's best if this signal conveys, or starts to convey, the Propositional Benefit. That happens when we *start* with the Propositional Benefit or use a Laid-On Benefit that gets the pause and also helps us deliver the Propositional Benefit with extra impact, clarity, and/or memorability. However, for a nanosecond, the advertisement might get that pause with the signaled appeal of a Laid-On Benefit that does *not* relate directly to the Propositional Benefit (but *is* compatible with the Propositional Benefit). *If* the advertisement uses such a Laid-On Benefit, it must segue *immediately* into the Propositional Benefit.

Immediately after the pause, the headline and major illustration (if any) must make readers *stop*—with the Propositional Benefit now in focus. We understand that what readers *first comprehend* becomes, *de facto*, what the advertisement proposes. Hence, what readers first comprehend must be what we *intended* to propose (the "A"). At this point, it's as though the reader has said, "OK, I know what you want to propose. Now lay it on me."

C. The advertisement typography, illustrations, layout, and amount of copy must give readers the *impression* that it will be relatively quick and easy to understand the entire proposition. And that must *prove to be the case*. Every element of the advertisement must work to make the proposition quickly, easily, and fully clear. Or easily and fully but not quickly provided it's all interesting (i.e., beneficial) to readers. At this point, it's as though readers weigh what you want them to do against the degree of interest they have in knowing all you want to communicate, and decide either, "Fair enough," or "Too much bother."

Then the Free Skating

In this area, I offered **The Creative Flow Chart**, with Approaches, Strategies, and Tactics for greatness in print advertising. Using the Flow Chart:

- We must make a pragmatic evaluation to decide whether we have a Great Proposition or a Routine Proposition. Whichever we have, our advertisement must exhibit certain qualities in Content (*Go with the tide*), Execution (*Get to the point*), and Tone (*Understand/like people*).
- If we have a Great Proposition, we take Approach 1, deciding that our Creative Approach will be *factual*, our Creative Strategy will be to make the Proposition *quickly*, *easily*, and *fully clear*, and our Creative Tactic will be *Creatively Non-Creative*. The last means being professional enough not to *set out* to play around and risk beclouding our clarity. But, while working for clarity, if something "clever" comes to us and does not subtract one whit from clarity, we will use it...happily.
- If we have a Routine Proposition, we will take Approach 2-A or 2-B or 2-C, in which we attempt to use great Emotion or Logic or Showmanship or Conviction or Trust or OK Competitiveness. Now we work in a try-and-succeed or try-and-fail-so-try-something-else fashion. First, we see if we can Increase INTEREST in our Routine Proposition by using one of the Creative Tactics that *reposition* it so people *perceive* a proposition somehow stronger than the one we actually make (Approach 2-A). If that doesn't work, we see if we can Increase Meaningful ATTENTION (increased attention to the Proposition) by using one of the Creative Tactics which do that (Approach 2-B). And, while we're working, it might come to us that we can both Increase INTEREST and Increase Meaningful ATTENTION by using a combination of Creative Tactics (Approach 2-C).
- We understand that perhaps 90% of what we do requires skillful application of *known* principles, techniques, and methods. So we don't just sit there hoping for what we call inspiration to strike from Lord knows where. We get to work considering/trying different Tactics to see which Strategy we can best follow. But we understand also that going the last 10% (or so)

demands an indefinable "leap of talent." Hence, we might not make it. Still, if we go that 90%, we will have something very close to great.

- If we do get all the way to a great print advertisement, we will have a Great *Advertising* Result (great attention to, interest in, and consideration and acceptance of our proposition).
- But then the marketing people must assure a Great *Marketing* Result (action on the Proposition).

For a CHECKLIST to assure no mistakes in the compulsories, and a Scoring System to critique "the free skating" part of an advertisement, please see the Appendix.

APPENDIX

CHECKLIST
for the A, B & C
of Effective
    Print Advertising
with SCORING SYSTEM
    for Approaches,
        Strategies,
    and Tactics
        to Reach Greatness

Introductory Notes

1. When using the **CHECKLIST** part, here are the answers you may give and what they mean:

   YES: Means that, with as much objectivity as you can muster, you see that element correctly executed. For Effective Print Advertising, you want all "YES" answers. (Though sometimes, for good reason, you may write "NO, BUT"—see below.)

   YES, BUT: Means the question can be answered "YES," but you think (or know) that whatever the question applies to can be done better.

   NO: Reveals *where* work needs to be done; and helps define specifically *what* must be done to make it right.

   NO, BUT: Means the element does *not* meet the standard for the rule, but there is an overriding reason to leave it as is.

   NA: Means the question is Not Applicable to that advertisement.

2. The objective of the CHECKLIST is to get you to take an advertisement apart, examine each element in isolation without regard to the rest of the advertisement and to critique each element by specific standards.

3. Deliberately, a degree of redundancy has been built into the CHECKLIST so that if you miss a fault in answering one question, you will likely catch it in answering one or more other questions.

4. When using the **SCORING SYSTEM** part, rate each item 1 to 10. For truly Great Print Advertising, work to improve any element for which you cannot justify a 10. A print advertisement must get straight 10's to qualify as great.

One Caution, Then Go For It I do not—repeat, do *not*—recommend trying to use this CHECKLIST and SCORING SYSTEM during a meeting. I cannot imagine agency creative or account people doing it (they would die first, I'm sure). And, if you're an MBA product manager, you will only confirm snide remarks about you doing everything by the book. I know the creative team always wants a reaction "right then and there" (and, having so often been on that side, I empathize with them). But I advocate critiquing copy and layout *in private first*; and *then* meeting when everyone is prepared to discuss—and capable of discussing—specific points with *as much specificity and objectivity as humanly possible.* After many, many overly long, vacuously and emotionally argumentative review meetings, I wrote this CHECKLIST and SCORING SYSTEM—and have used it for years—precisely for such preparation.

CHECKLIST: The A, B & C of Effective Print Advertising

A. An *effective* print advertisement offers the strongest possible Propositional Benefit to the largest possible number of the right people. And the visually strongest—thus first seen—element of the advertisement is compatible with that Proposition.

(**NOTE:** What readers *comprehend first*—with only an idle, mind-absent glance—becomes, *de facto*, THE Proposition. (Note the difference between "*see* first" and "*comprehend* first.") Therefore, answer all the questions in this "A" section in relation to what readers will first comprehend, not in terms of what may be "down in the copy.")

1 ___ **In every conceivable way, does what people first comprehend start from where most readers are in relationship to the product, service, company, organization, or cause at this time? Also, does it start from where they are in relation to advertising in general?**

2 ___ Is the overall "look" of the advertisement compatible with the Proposition it will make?

3 ___ Especially in style, but also in content, is the major illustration, if any, compatible with the Proposition that the advertisement will make?

    3A ___ In content, pose, and style, does the major illustration, if any, avoid being a typical, "overacted," silly advertisement illustration?

4 ___ Does what readers will comprehend first offer what many people want most (or at least very much) in or from that category of product or service *at this time*?

5 ___ If offering a new kind of product—or any new product—does the headline relate that new product to an *already existing interest* of many people?

6 ___ If aimed at people NOT now doing/believing what the advertisement proposes, does the headline deal with a common reason why they don't?

7 ___ If aimed primarily at current users or "believers," does it work to reinforce their "good judgment"?

8 ___ If aimed at current users of a product or service, does it work to get people to use more...or to use it better?

9 ___ If aimed primarily at NEW users, does it offer what most people might consider a good reason to "switch" or to start for the first time to use what is advertised?

10 ___ (**Corporate Advertising**) Does the headline reveal a sensitive empathy with how most people feel about the company and/or the industry *at this time*?

11 ___ (**Advocacy Advertising**) Does it urge doing or believing what you can reasonably expect many people to do or believe *at this time*?

12 ___ If the headline asks a question, is it one many people logically might ask *at this time* ... or really care to have answered at all?

    12A ___ If the headline asks a question, is it asked in the vernacular all those people out there would use in asking it?

13 ___ If the headline asks a question, is it one to which people could expect an objective answer from that particular advertiser?

14 ___ If the headline asks a question that readers are supposed to answer for or about themselves, is it one the answer to which will in *no way* embarrass people or make them feel awkward?

15 ___ If the headline offers to explain something, is it something many people might care to have explained *at this time* or ever?

16 __ If the headline or major illustration is trying to be humorous, does it come off? If trying to be clever, will people "get it"?

    16A __ If the headline is trying a play on words, does it end up "saying" what was intended to be said?

    16B __ If the headline is trying to be clever does it avoid a "creative faux pas" that destroys the effect?

B. Even when given only an idle, mind-absent glance, an *effective* print advertisement instantly signals *some* benefit to readers (i.e., readers quickly/easily see or sense some reason for them to *pause*). Either simultaneously or instantly after, it brings that benefit into sharp enough focus to make them *stop*. (If what you use to make them pause is not the Propositional Benefit, the advertisement quickly and easily brings the Propositional Benefit into focus.)

17 __ Will just idle glancing reveal any reason(s) to pause...possibly to stop?

If the advertisement uses a Laid-On Benefit:

18 __ Will people understand it quickly and will it interest them enough to make them pause?

19 __ Does it start to deliver the Propositional Benefit or, if not, does it permit a quick and easy segue into it?

20 __ Does it avoid being just a silly, senseless gimmick or even one that can actually work *against* the advertisement's proposition?

21 __ Does it avoid dominating the advertisement to the extent that people might remember the Laid-On Benefit but not the Propositional Benefit?

Whether the advertisement uses either the Propositional Benefit or a Laid-On Benefit to get people to pause... possibly stop:

22 __ Does the advertisement have an active (even if calm), "trying to tell you something" look (as opposed to a static, "cast in concrete" appearance)?

23 __ Will the overall "look" of the advertisement (created by the colors, the layout, the content/style of illustrations, key headline words, and the typography) signal that "something interesting (i.e., of possible benefit) to reader" is being said/shown?

24 __ If the overall "look" of the advertisement is chichi or in some way esoteric, does it still "say" something understandable (even if non-verbal) and benefit-suggesting to the people at whom it is aimed?

25 __ (**Response Advertisement**— coupon, direct marketing, promotion): Does the overall "look" instantly say, "this advertisement wants a response"?

26 __ Will the layout of the advertisement pull readers' eyes to where they *should* go first—to where they will see or sense some reason to pause?

27 ___ If the headline is supposed to be a "teaser," will most people understand it enough to either (1) have their curiosity aroused or (2) be prepared for the "payoff"?

28 ___ If the headline or major illustration is trying to be clever, does it still quickly/clearly offer a benefit (Propositional or Laid-On)—some reason to pause?

29 ___ Will certain key words of the headline likely touch a strong, already existing interest of many readers?

    29A ___ Is the headline broken/stacked to make such key words stand out? (Think of Dynamic Headlining.)

    29B ___ Will those key words help to make at least the essence, if not the facts, of the Propositional Benefit quickly/easily recognizable?

30 ___ Will the style or content of the artwork signal benefit to most readers, giving them reason—even if vague—to pause?

    30A ___ Will the style or content of the artwork help to make at least the essence if not the facts of the Propositional Benefit quickly/easily recognizable?

After an *effective* advertisement gets people to *pause*, it gets them to *stop* with (1) a headline so easy to speed-read and understand that people might easily read and understand it even before they "decide" to try (or certainly with no effort) and (2) illustration(s) equally quick and easy to understand. And both headline and illustration(s) work to make the Propositional Benefit quickly/easily clear; or to lead into the quick/easy segue from a Laid-On Benefit to the Propositional Benefit.

31 ___ **Is the headline easy—EASY— to speed-read?**

32 ___ Does the headline use familiar combinations of words in a familiar sequence?

33 ___ Or, if it deliberately uses UN-familiar words or sequences, will people easily understand the "word game" being played, thus, with equal ease, understand quickly/correctly what the headline "says"?

34 ___ Does the headline use an easily readable typeface, set in an easily readable way?

    34A ___ Is the headline to be printed in a way that will make it very easy to read?

35 ___ If the headline contains more than a few words, is it broken into two or more lines?

    35A ___ If so, are the lines broken and stacked for easiest speed-reading?

    35B ___ Is the headline set as a Dynamic Headline? (This is not a "must," but consider the possible advantage.)

36 ___ If there is no headline, is at least the opening copy (better yet, *all* of the copy) set large enough (14 or more points) and in such an

easily readable way that people will likely "slide" into reading before they consciously decide to begin?

    36A ___ And is every sentence written in such a way that it pulls you on to the next . . . and the next . . . and the next . . . right to the end?

37 ___ **Is the art easy to understand?**

38 ___ Does the artwork use familiar objects in a familiar pattern?

39 ___ Or, if the artwork deliberately uses familiar objects in an UNfamiliar pattern, are people likely to understand the "art game" that is being played...or what it is trying to "show" or "say." Are they, thus, likely to quickly/easily understand the artwork correctly?

40 ___ Is the artwork to be printed in such a way that will help make it quickly/easily understandable?

41 ___ **(Response Advertisement):** Is the coupon, order form, or entry form instantly recognizable as such? Is it an artistic cliché? (Rectangular, surrounded by dash lines, etc. In this case, we *want* a cliché because that makes the coupon instantly recognized.)

    41A ___ **(Response Advertisement):** Is the coupon, entry form, or order form where it should be—in the lower outside corner or all along the bottom?

42 ___ **(Response Advertisement):** Is the coupon, order form, or entry form as visually strong as it can be?

C. After an *effective* **print advertisement gets people to pause and to stop, during that pause and stop, every element of the advertisment works to make the Propositional Benefit quickly, easily, and fully understood:**

43 ___ **On an "Index of Comprehension," will idle glancing move readers off zero in the right direction?**

44 ___ Does the first impression of the advertisement (gained from color, layout, style and content of illustration(s), typography, AND easily seen key headline words that are readable at a glance) start to move readers off zero toward 100 positive?

45 ___ Are you sure the first impression does not move readers off zero in the wrong direction?

46 ___ **(Response Advertisement):** Does the first impression start to "say" money off, order here (and now), enter the contest (or whatever the promotion)?

    46A ___ **(Response Advertisement):** Is the layout style appropriate to the purpose of the advertisement?

47 ___ **Does the headline and/or major illustration get right to work helping to make the Proposition fully clear?**

48 ___ Does the headline start actually to deliver the Proposition?

48A ___ Or at least, does it "say" something that orients readers so that they can easily understand the Proposition from the rest of the advertisement?

49 ___ Or, if essentially a visual advertisement, does the major illustration start to deliver the Proposition?

49A ___ Or at least, does it show something that orients readers so that they can easily understand the Proposition from the rest of the advertisement?

50 ___ (**Response Advertisement**): Does the headline make the offer, announce the promotion, or in some way make clear what the advertisement seeks as a response?

50A ___ (**Response Advertisement**): Does the headline make it quickly and easily clear (1) what is being offered and (2) for what action by or payment from responders?

50B ___ (**Response Advertisement**): Does the advertisement (headline, copy, and illustrations) help make it *look* easy (then actually *make* it easy) to respond RELATIVE to how much they are likely to want what is offered?

51 ___ **Do the headline and major illustration work together to help make the Proposition fully clear?**

52 ___ Because eyes generally go first to an illustration, to make the headline and illustration work together like a fast one-two punch, the art must be *instantly* understandable. *Is it?*

53 ___ Is the relationship between the headline and illustration instantly understandable?

54 ___ **Is the advertisement easy to "follow"?**

55 ___ **Is the copy easy to read?**

55A ___ Is it written in a conversational, easy-to-scan-read style?

55B ___ Does it use an easy-to-read typeface set in an easy-to-read way?

56 ___ **Is the copy brief relative to the value (to most people) of the Propositional Benefit and/or relative to how much most people generally want to know about your category of product or service or about your company or cause?**

57 ___ If the Proposition can be made quickly and easily—and also fully clear—with only a headline and illustration, does the advertisement do that?

58 ___ With allowance for some repetition in advertising, if the opening copy repeats the headline or subhead (if any), is the repetition really necessary?

59 ___ Does the copy start with what is most likely new (but understandable) to most people—not wasting words saying what they already know?

60 ___ Do the sentences and paragraphs run in a straight-line sequence, free of "detours"?

61 ___ Again with allowance for some repetition in advertising, is the *body* of the copy free of unnecessary repetition?

62 ___ Does the copy use mainly active verbs?

63 ___ If any claims need documentation, does the copy give only as much as reasonably needed?

64 ___ Is the copy free of windy phrases that can be replaced with a word or two?

65 ___ If the copy contains any positive/negative statements (e.g., It's not difficult, it's easy.) are both positive and negative really needed?

66 ___ Is the copy free of extreme widow lines? (With typeset copy, cutting just one or two such widows amounts to the same as cutting a full line.)

67 ___ Is the copy free of impractical exhortations?

68 ___ Once again, granting the sometime value of repetition in advertising, if the copy ends by repeating the propositional point, is that repetition really needed?

69 ___ Have you taken every possible opportunity to use an explanatory picture/caption in place of quite a few words?

70 ___ Does the copy *stop* when it has no more of value (to readers) to say?

71 ___ **Does the advertisement make best use of its square inches (1) to be as visually strong as possible and (2) for maximum communications within its space limitation?**

72 ___ Does it drop out or crop off unnecessary parts of the art?

72A ___ Does it take full advantage of the visual power gained by close-in cropping?

73 ___ Does it drop out unnecessary background to make illustrated objects stand out?

74 ___ If possible without hurting easy readability, does it make multiple use of the same space (e.g. headline over a plain, dark part of the illustration)?

75 ___ Does it use the bleed space?

75A ___ Is art placed on the outer sides of the layout to make that possible?

76 ___ Does it use boldface paragraph lead-ins instead of centered, separate copy subheads?

77 ___ Is the copy set in no more than two columns per page?

78 ___ Unless a border is needed for some important reason, is the advertisement UNbordered?

Scoring System to move from Effective to Great starts next page.

SCORING SYSTEM for Approaches, Strategies and Tactics to Reach Greatness

(Reminder: Score 1 to 10, and a great print advertisement will get straight 10's.)

79 ___ In content, the advertisement must go with the tide.

80 ___ In execution, it must hit hard, fast, and home.

    80A ___ If it signals that it will *not* hit fast, it must immediately signal an acceptable-to-readers reason why.

81 ___ In tone, the advertisement must be friendly and "on the reader's side."

    81A ___ The advertisement must reflect a sincere interest in people (even if humorous or a little flip) as opposed to being entirely self-centered and "ady."

    81B ___ In total "feeling" (wording and illustration), the advertisement must be courteous as opposed to pugnacious and/or antagonistic.

    81C ___ If somehow delicate, the subject must be handled with what most people will consider good taste.

82 ___ If the advertisement has a Great Proposition:

- Its Creative Approach should be factual.

- Its Creative Strategy should be to make the Proposition quickly, easily, fully, and memorably clear.

- Its Creative Tactic should be to be Creatively NON-Creative.

    82A ___ Sometimes, with a Great Proposition that will get high interest and attention if simply "said and shown," it may be possible to use one of the Creative Tactics that Increase INTEREST or Increase Meaningful ATTENTION even more.

83 ___ If the advertisement must work with a Routine Proposition:

- Its Creative Approach must be to employ great Emotion, Logic, Showmanship, Conviction, Trust, or OK Competitiveness.

- Its Creative Strategy must be to Increase INTEREST or Increase Meaningful ATTENTION or both.

- It must use one or more of the Creative Tactics to achieve either or both of those results. Score the degree of skill/artistry with which Tactic or Tactics are used.

Increase INTEREST
____ Justified Pride
____ You Can Do It . . . Easily
____ Repeated Great Line
____ Short Short Story
____ Walter Mitty
____ Proposition Challenge
____ Go Beyond Product Features
____ Personify
____ "Quiet" Statement
____ Testimonial
____ It's OK To Do
____ That Makes Sense
____ Yes, That's True
____ Profitable Public Service
____ Heaven Forbid!
____ Other

Increase Meaningful ATTENTION
____ Oh, I Get It!
____ Ink/Paper Special Effects
____ GOTCHA!
____ Word Play—Clever/Clear
____ Acceptable Exaggeration
____ Quick/Easy Game
____ VOILA!
____ Vivid Visualization
____ Hey, I'm Talking To You!
____ Kids And Dogs
____ Other

Additional Permission Notices

The following advertisements were used with permission, as noted.

Advertisement in margin on page 48: With permission of Timex Corp.

Advertisement on page 53: With permission of Del Monte Foods, Inc.

Advertisement at bottom of page 54: With permission of Delta Faucet Co.

Advertisement on page 56: With permission of U.S. Postal Service

Advertisement at bottom of page 58: With permission of Nabisco Brands, Inc.

Index